THE KURAL

THE KURAL

Tiruvalluvar's Tirukkural

TRANSLATED FROM THE TAMIL BY

THOMAS HITOSHI PRUIKSMA

Beacon Press
Boston

BEACON PRESS
Boston, Massachusetts
www.beacon.org

Beacon Press books
are published under the auspices of
the Unitarian Universalist Association of Congregations.

Printed in the United States of America

24 23 22 21 8 7 6 5 4 3 2 1

This book is printed on acid-free paper
that meets the uncoated paper ANSI/NISO
specifications for permanence as revised in 1992.

Text design by Michael Starkman
at Wilsted & Taylor Publishing Services

Library of Congress Cataloging-in-Publication Data

Names: Tiruvaḷḷuvar, author. | Pruiksma, Thomas H., translator.
Title: The kural : Tiruvalluvar's Tirukkural /
translated from the Tamil by Thomas Hitoshi Pruiksma.
Other titles: Tirukkuṛaḷ. English
Description: Boston : Beacon Press, [2021]
Identifiers: LCCN 2021030420 (print) | LCCN 2021030421 (ebook) |
ISBN 9780807003619 (hardcover ; acid-free paper) |
ISBN 9780807003626 (ebook)
Subjects: LCSH: Tiruvaḷḷuvar—Translations into English. |
Tamil poetry—To 1500—Translations into English. | LCGFT: Poetry.
Classification: LCC PL4758.9.T5 T513 2021 (print) |
LCC PL4758.9.T5 (ebook) | DDC 894.8/1111—dc23
LC record available at https://lccn.loc.gov/2021030420
LC ebook record available at https://lccn.loc.gov/2021030421

For the late Dr. K. V. Ramakoti,
beloved teacher,
mentor, and friend

CONTENTS

III. RENUNCIATION

IV. FATE

PART TWO WEALTH

I. SOVEREIGNTY

II. THE ARMS OF GOVERNMENT

III. ALL ELSE

PART THREE LOVE

I. SECRET LOVE

II. WEDDED LOVE

FOREWORD

Anyone who is, even unwillingly, half awake knows with increasing dread and anguish that the whole world now is plunged into an unprecedented many-layered crisis that threatens the whole human adventure. The coronavirus rages, the Amazon burns, the polar ice melts, a million species totter on the brink of extinction, the chasm between rich and poor is expanding, and billionaires flourish while middle-class and blue-collar workers line up for food; democracy all over the world is threatened by authoritarianism and the spread of outrageous conspiracy theories, what Barack Obama refers to, too politely, as "global truth decay" but which should really be named "truth genocide."

An old priest I love in Chidambaram, the greatest of all Shivite temples in Tamil Nadu, said to me last year, "We are now at a late stage of Kali Yuga, the age when the Dark One dances and all things are potentially destroyed. The human race will either die out, and soon, or transform completely under the pressure of extreme tragedy and birth a new kind of human being in harmony with God and so able to co-create a new world."

Three years before I had been in Australia, attending the Dalai Lama's teachings on the tantra of transfiguration in the Tibetan Vajrayana tradition. For days his holiness poured out precise transcendent wisdom in a stark cement room draped with Tibetan tangkas. In a corridor after the last session, I had the opportunity to ask him a question.

"Do you think humanity will survive?"

He paused and said quietly, "I do not know. No one knows." Then, he smiled. "Prepare for the worst, and work tirelessly for the best."

Those who work tirelessly for the best—the birth of a new kind of human being and a new world rising like a phoenix out of the smoldering ashes of the old—know one thing. They know that our greatest hope, encouragement, and inspiration will come not from our contemporary, absurdly narcissistic "New Age" spirituality, nor from the religions in their state of decay, nor from science or from economics nor political change, but from the treasure houses of spiritual wisdom that mature ancient civilizations offer us. The enlightened testimony of the great sages—from Lao-Tzu to Buddha to Jesus and Rumi and Kabir, and in our time, Anandamayi Ma, Ramana Maharshi, and Sri Aurobindo—offers us the peace and rigor of timeless truth as the foundation of the one life worth living at any time, but especially in this one. And that is a life surrendered to the Divine, loving and serving its laws of compassion to, and justice for, all, whatever the hell or heaven happens. This birthing force of a new humanity is what I have called "sacred activism," an activism grounded in, inspired, and guided by divine consciousness. In the last century, we have seen what "impossible" transformations can be initiated by human beings such as Gandhi, Nelson Mandela, Martin Luther King Jr., Jane Goodall, and the Dalai Lama, who enshrine and enact this truth.

This is where the majestic masterpiece of South Indian civilization, the Kural, written centuries ago, comes in. Its author, Tiruvalluvar, is not only one of India's but one of the world's greatest poets, a master of the couplet aphorism, the most naked and exigent of forms. He is a sage of sacred life, and his vision of a world flooded with divine presence and governed by divine laws, whose observance engenders joy, balance, and harmony for all beings, could not be more relevant or inspiring for us, or more essential, not only to admire, but to learn from.

I was born in 1952 in Coimbatore, Tamil Nadu, and spent the first nine years of my childhood there and in Delhi. For three years of my childhood, from six to nine, I was educated in its Nilgiri Hills, where my parents now lie buried.

In the forty years since, Tamil Nadu has been the secret center of my mystical unfolding. Since the moment I first encountered the Kural—in a visit to Tamil Nadu at age twenty-eight, in the sometimes garbled translations by G. U. Pope—I have revered and read and reread it. Astonished afresh at each rereading, I found my own inner experience expanded and revealed to me not only as a sublime crystallization of the wisdom of ancient Indian civilization but also, miraculously, as an ever-fresh guide to any serious efforts to birth, out of the apocalyptic chaos of our Kali ordeal, a new world. Long revered among the Tamils as a book to live and die by, the Kural deserves now to be read by seekers everywhere and by all those who know that, in André Malraux's words, "the twenty-first century will either be founded on a mystical foundation, or not at all."

The Kural offers us nothing less than a balanced and precise vision of how to live, love, work, and flourish in an already sacred world, a world known and recognized to be entirely sacred in all of its realms, both transcendent and immanent. It invites us calmly and with both ruthless and exalted authority to celebrate this sacred reality and respect its laws in every activity and domain of our lives, or risk our destruction, and the destruction of the creation it is our responsibility to protect. The Kural could only have been written by an enlightened being. In the astonishingly fresh and vibrant translations that adorn this book, Tiruvalluvar's voice can now reach the universal audience that so deeply needs its universal wisdom.

In honor of these translations and this wisdom, I have chosen eleven of the Kural's aphorisms in an unfolding order, with commentary. May this order and my commentary inspire you in your own exploration of and meditation on Tiruvalluvar's message, and grace you the sober joy and resolution it continues to grace me.

350 Hold to the hold of one who holds nothing—to hold nothing
Hold to that hold

All the great mystical traditions know that the ultimate reality that creates and permeates everything can only be, inadequately, expressed as "nothing"—the "Ayin" of the kabbalists, the "Nirguna Brahman" of Hinduism, the "Sunya" or "Void" of Buddhism, Islam's "Allah" (one of whose meanings is the No-Thing), the "Tao" of Taoists, the "Godhead" of the Christian mystics, from Meister Eckhart to Saint John of the Cross, Kabir's "Unshadowed God."

It is in holding to the One that is this "Nothing"—or to one who, initiated into the final mystery of this One, holds to "Nothing"—that we gradually unlearn everything, both the concepts of the ego and the dogmas, however illumined, of religion. Then we can live in that "unknowing knowing" that, over time, liberates and transfigures us (as Kabir would say "engoldens" us) in eternal life.

This, as Tiruvalluvar knows, is the secret of secrets, the secret that has revolutionized forever the lives of all humanity's greatest evolutionary pioneers, from the Jewish prophets to Jesus and Mohammed, from Lao-Tzu to Aurobindo and the Dalai Lama, and countless other seekers through the ages who have discovered its all-transforming alchemy.

30 Those who let go embody grace—they show
Compassion to all

Those who "let go"—surrender wholly to the mystery by "holding to the one who holds nothing"—are transfigured by grace in mind, heart, and body. The sign that this alchemy of "engoldenment" is real in you is that "you show compassion to all," to the evil as well as the good, and not only to human beings but also, as Tiruvalluvar makes clear throughout the Kural, to animals and all other sentient beings. This compassion is not what Chogyam Trungpa Rinpoche called "idiot compassion." It is united with discerning wisdom that sees and knows all things and beings in their complex interrelation, and that faces the devastation that dark choices spread with illusionless rigor.

1073 The wicked are like gods—they too
Do as they please

This devastating couplet enshrines the profound discerning wisdom that divine compassion is one with. It demonstrates with ironic precision why evil is seductive: abolishing or flouting conscience offers a pseudo-godlike freedom of action and possibility, while "holding to the one who holds nothing" demands stringent discipline and clinging to truth. Tiruvalluvar here reveals, in a few brief words, why so many in our time, unmoored from sacred revelation, have chosen the path of dark power, with the apocalyptic consequences we see now threatening the human race with extinction. This famous couplet is at once a warning to those who love God to struggle to make this shadow conscious so they can "embody grace" and a subtle warning to the wicked who, while they may imagine they are "free," are only "like" gods, doomed to be destroyed through karmic payback for their actions.

1072 The wicked are luckier than the good—nothing
Troubles their hearts

Those who choose what Kabir calls "the hard, winding, thorny road" to embodying grace will be subjected to many fierce ordeals as the price of being born into a new reality. Those who choose the dark will seem to be luckier; their stone hearts will not be ravaged by the multiple heartbreaks that break again and again the hearts of the good. This "luck" is illusory. To not be "troubled" by ordeal or by the agony of the world bars the wicked from transformation and so ensures their continual rebirth in illusion.

72 Everything belongs to the loveless—for the loving
Bones too belong to others

The price to enter the stream of embodying grace is the act of dying to the nature of the false self that, in its lethal narcissism, is loveless, addicted to the fantasy that everything exists for its use and pleasure. It is this fantasy of the loveless that we can now clearly see ruining the planet in an orgy of greed. Those who divine love transfigures, however, lose all illusions of separation: divine wisdom and divine compassion unite in them to make them what the great Christian mystic Hadewijch of Antwerp called "slaves of love." They know they are "others" and "others" are them: their lives are consumed willingly in the fire of relentless service to all beings.

95 Humility and sweet speech adorn one in beauty—
All else does not

Those who embody grace radiate humility, the humility of true knowledge, and speak their truth with a tender precision and respect that has the best hope of winning and transforming hearts. The beauty that adorns them is the mysterious beauty of God who "is beauty and loves the beautiful," as the Koran proclaims. The true aim of human life, Tiruvalluvar says, is not wealth or power or success but to become "beautiful," to be transfigured by love into its humble and radiant servant.

597 Even stung by arrows the elephant stands tall—even stung
By failure the sturdy do not slacken

It would be a mistake to imagine that Tiruvalluvar's ideal is a passive one. The beauty that the previous couplet celebrates is founded in adamantine strength. As my great teacher, Father Bede Griffiths, once said to me, "The divine human being is, at once, tender as a flower and hard as a diamond."

In its deepest sense, the Kural is a training in nobility of the soul. Only those forged in the soul's noble furnace will be able to continue telling truth to power and standing up for justice and compassion. Rugged hope is implied in Tiruvalluvar's words. If the sturdy and noble do not slacken when assaulted and defeated again and again, not only will they themselves embody grace but grace itself, in its own timing, may realize their selfless dreams for humanity.

26 The great do the impossible—the small do
What everyone can

Those who die nobly in life into eternal truth are capable, through the mystery of grace, of doing what seems impossible, of being nothing less than living channels of miraculous grace. All authentic mystical traditions know and celebrate this revelation, and ignorance of its reality is one reason contemporary humanity suffers so deeply from meaninglessness, apathy, and despair.

In our time, when so many living beings are clearly threatened with extinction, true lovers of God must strive for this greatness, the greatness of the beautiful and sturdy who embody grace. Without its empowerment, collaboration with the evolutionary will of the Divine to birth a new humanity out of the death of the old is impossible; with it, there are no human limits to what the divine can accomplish through the human being surrendered to its love.

675 Bring these five out of darkness and act—
Tools time place means deed

The beautiful and sturdy who become living channels of miraculous grace do impossible things: their actions radiate divine blessing and divine power.

In a time as dire as ours, it is only this vision of sacredly inspired and embodied truth in action that can possibly save us. Those who know this, who "bring these five out of darkness" and know their "bones too belong to others," and continue to act for compassion and justice, are transfigured themselves and pioneer the birth of a transfigured humanity and world.

In its few words, this couplet sums up this birthing force of sacred action. We need the appropriate tools to become empowered and the patience and wisdom to know when they can be employed, as well as the place to use them. Skillful means are required of us; we must be attuned to the situation. The deed itself is the precise divinely guided and ordained action that can realize the tools' combined power. To those who surrender wholly to the will of God and embody grace, the interfusion of "tools time place means deed" becomes effortless. It makes seemingly impossible individual and structural changes in our world possible.

367 Undying deeds happen as hoped if one severs
Desire completely

The condition for becoming an instrument of transformative sacred action and a humble transfigured pioneer of a new humanity and world is the surrender of the fruits of action to the divine. All authentic mystical systems proclaim this truth, and realizing it demands the ultimate ascesis of sacrificial patience and surrender. The reward of this ascesis is that "undying deeds happen as hoped"—that the "hope" all sacred activists keep alive in their hearts and struggle to enact in their actions, while surrendering the timing of its realization to the Divine does, when the Divine wills it, not only flowers but flowers in a way far richer and more powerful than anything they could have imagined. This is the one message of the Gita, of the Gospels, of the Mahayana scriptures, of Lao-Tzu and Sri Aurobindo, and it is the message those of us who refuse to give up on humanity in its hour of greatest danger most need to steady and direct their lives.

382 Generosity fearlessness knowledge energy—the nature
of a king
Is these four in fullness

To be an authentic sacred activist is to be "royal," to embody the grace of the sturdy and beautiful in selfless action for the Divine and the divine in humanity. This couplet, with sublime brilliance, demonstrates what qualities the "royal" sacred activist needs to cultivate and fuse together in their separate and interconnected fullness: generosity and magnanimity in all situations; freedom from fear born from surrender to the One, and the profound and deathless self-knowledge it graces; the passionate and compassionate energy that intense devotion to God engenders, inflames, and sustains.

What is especially revealing in this couplet and in Tiruvalluvar's description of his "royal" ideal is the emphasis he places on "energy" by putting it last. Far too often, a half-baked understanding of Indian spirituality, including by Indians themselves, has exalted a passive renunciation over the dynamic one that makes a rich and full divine human life possible. For Tiruvalluvar, as I have tried to show throughout this commentary, life is God's field of transfiguration, and the human being is potentially a living channel of active miraculous grace.

It is this glorious and universally empowering vision that irradiates all aspects of the Kural and makes it an indispensable guide for our time. We will either continue in our blind and savage addictions and die out, or risk the adventure the Kural celebrates: embody grace and co-create with the Divine a new humanity and a new world. The choice is ours.

ANDREW HARVEY

This introduction is dedicated to my beloved friend
and co-conspirator Ellen Gunter,
who embodies sturdy and beautiful grace.

INTRODUCTION

An Unbiased Heart Adorns Wisdom: Some Thoughts on the Tirukkural *

I grew up with the Tirukkural, but not in the way you might think. I did not learn its couplets by heart, nor have appropriate verses cited to me to teach me how to be properly Tamil: good, generous, modest. Rather, for this urban, English-educated, middle-class girl, it hovered in the background, lacing my childhood memories: Tirukkural verses on public transport buses, startling white against the sage-green drawing the eye, a curling Tamil script, incomprehensible to me, illiterate in the language, and next to it, in florid Roman and turgid English, an utterly opaque translation; rumbling past the busy intersection at the city center, sighting the mute, unsmiling, forbidding statue of the poem's author rooted at the entrance of the Sanskrit College; another granite-black statue of the author with the sea at his back; a huge chariot monument honoring the poet and his poem, looming over an arterial node at the heart of the city; hearing the poem's famous first couplet open the popular Tamil films of K. Balachander (1930–2014) and singing along with it; being told the tale of the needle the poet placed by his banana leaf to pick up stray rice that might spill while he ate or when his wife, Vāsuki, served him his meal—he never needed it, for neither wasted a single grain of rice; serve like her and eat like him, was the implication. These were formative experiences of the Tirukkural, which embedded itself within me as boring, stodgy, preachy,

---

* This is an excerpt from the second half of a famous kural:

> *kēṭum perukkamum illalla neñcattuk*
> *kōṭamai cāṉṟōrkku aṇi* (115)

Translated by Thomas Pruiksma as:

> Rising and falling have never not been—an unbiased heart
> Adorns wisdom

and didactic. I could not fathom its power nor understand the ferocious affection it engendered in lovers of Tamil. I eventually got there, as a mentor predicted I would, taken in by the Kural's economical form and the enduring wisdom of its content. With this revelation, late though it came, I was simply joining legions of readers, listeners, and commentators, really, *enthusiasts*, of this eminently quotable meditation on ethics and a well-lived life. A few citations, apt for our times, make the point:

40 Action that fits is virtue—action
That doesn't is vice

83 The life that cherishes strangers each day
Never falls upon ruin

105 Help does not measure help—the heart of the helped
Measures help

119 Fairness means speech without bias—when bias
Is absent within*

Whether inscribed on buses or memorized and quoted, Kural verses such as these have come to be understood as fundamental expressions of Tamil-ness. Centuries of commentaries and the more recent flood of translations into multiple languages have cemented the link between this ancient text and modern conceptions of Tamil identity. Thus interwoven, especially in the past one hundred years, into the very fabric of what it means to be Tamil, it is impossible to separate the Kural from its reception and the long, teeming rivers of receptive histories, into which Thomas Pruiksma's exquisite translation now merges itself.

One might say the Tirukkural has two trajectories of reception that have cemented its place as an iconic Tamil text and as a jewel of world literature. In the first is its laudatory status within the Tamil literary tradition as *tamil maṟai* (Revealed Tamil), *poyyāmoḻi* (Speech without Falsity, i.e., unimpeachable truth), and *deyvanūl* (Divine Text),

* All translations in my introduction are by Thomas Pruiksma.

affirmed by the long history of available commentary on the text, beginning in the eleventh century and continuing into the twenty-first century. While ten commentaries are mentioned in a text called the *Peruntokai* (Great Collection), only five have survived.* In the Indic intellectual tradition, commentary is not merely about exegesis but equally about canonicity and an assertion of status for both author and text. So, if one wanted to be taken seriously as a Tamil scholar, you commented on the Tirukkural, its dense succinct couplets, its wordplay, the meditations on almost every aspect of life, providing the ideal canvas on which to sketch one's own imaginative reading and interpretation, and in doing so, asserting one's intellectual heft.

These commentaries, composed between the eleventh and thirteenth centuries—the peak period for Kural exposition—laid the strong foundations for the text's reception, even as the meaning of the text and the symbolism of its author changed to accommodate societal needs. In the absence of any definitive autobiographical information about the text's author and the text's apparently universalist ethics, medieval interpreters could shape it to their ends. For instance, Parimēlaḻakar (c. thirteenth century), the Kural's most famous commentator, was a Tamil Vaishnava brahmin, and his commentary, which liberally quotes from Tamil Vaishnava devotional literature, reflects these religious commitments, while European encounters with the poem, like that of the eminent nineteenth-century scholar and missionary G. U. Pope (1820–1908), read into it early Christian influence.

If commentary is the primary means of ensuring a text's longevity and canonicity, in the premodern and early modern periods, beginning in the eighteenth century, translation into European languages, arguably, comes to occupy that space.† Most of these translations, undertaken by Christian missionaries, were deliberately incomplete,

* These are the commentaries of Maṇakkuṭavar, Pariperumāḷ, Paritiyār, Parimēlaḻakar, and Kāliṅkar. The earliest commentary is that of Maṇakkuṭavar, while Parimēlaḻakar's is the latest and the most well known.

† The earliest extant translation of the Tirukkural appears to be into Malayalam in the late sixteenth century. Kamil Zvelebil, *Tamil Literature* (Leiden: E. J. Brill, 1975), 127n99.

choosing to leave out the book's vivid, sensuous third section devoted to love. Of these, the earliest was the 1730 Latin translation of Joseph Beschi (1680–1747), while the brilliant British civil servant Francis Whyte Ellis (1777–1819), who dedicated his life to the study of this text, left a partial English translation of 120 verses, published in 1812. A German translation by August Friedrich Caemmerer (1767–1837) came out in 1803, while E. S. Ariel (1818–1854) brought out a French translation in 1848. G. U. Pope, the influential nineteenth-century Christian missionary scholar mentioned above, published the first complete English translation of the Tirukkural in 1886.

Many of these translation efforts of the Kural emerged against the backdrop of debates about Tamil's literary history, even as the great U. V. Swaminatha Iyer (1855–1942) reintroduced long forgotten texts into the canon.* In the absence of access to these earlier works, early European encounters with Tamil deemed the Tirukkural the oldest extant Tamil literary work and marked it (inaccurately) as the beginning of Tamil literary production. Later research corrected this hypothesis. The Tirukkural is without question an early work, composed between the fourth and fifth centuries, some three centuries after the classical period of poetry, referred to as the Sangam Age.†

For such an important poem, we know surprisingly little about its origins or its author. E. S. Ariel, the nineteenth-century French translator of the Kural who pithily characterized the masterpiece, in a letter to a colleague, as a "book without a name by an author without a name."‡ The title Tirukkural simply refers to its metrical form (*the kural*), with the prefix *tiru* a marker of honor, sacrality, and reverence.

---

* For a discussion placing the Tirukkural within larger Tamil literary history, and about its translation and print history, see Zvelebil, *Tamil Literature*, 123–27, and David Shulman, *Tamil: A Biography* (Cambridge, MA: Harvard University Press, 2016), 91–98.

† The most important of these figures is Robert Caldwell (1814–1891), a Christian missionary, largely credited with identifying Tamil as belonging to the Dravidian language family. He regarded the Tirukkural to be Tamil literature's oldest work, which he dated erroneously to the tenth century.

‡ "Ce livre sans nom, par un auteur sans nom." Quoted in G. U. Pope, *The Sacred Kurral Tiruvalluva Nayanar* (London: W. H. Allen and Company, 1886), i.

There is nothing in the body of the Tirukkural about the poet—in a sense, he is utterly absent—allowing scholars to offer up various theories on his precise affiliation. Most scholars today agree that given his use of a distinctly Jain vocabulary for god and the text's emphasis on asceticism, that the author was likely a Jain.* So, the myth of the poet, and indeed his very name—Tiruvaḷḷuvar—emerges several centuries after the composition of his poem, sometime in the tenth or eleventh century, in a poem of fifty-three short verses called the *Tiruvaḷḷuva Mālai* (The Garland on Tiruvaḷḷuvar). Here too the information is scant. We only hear that the Tirukkural, tested at the Sangam Academy of Poets by pompous poets, bests all their petty verses and is divinely decreed as superior. This pivotal, albeit tropic, scene and the poet's name, Vaḷḷuvar, become the kernels around which the story of the poet and his famous poem are built.

The story of Vaḷḷuvar no doubt circulated in oral and folk forms prior to the nineteenth century, but it is during this period, under the power of a thriving print culture in Tamil country, that it begins to consolidate. The poet's name, Vaḷḷuvar, is itself the departure point for his legend, for it can mean weaver (*vaḷḷuvaṉ*) or can also refer to a special caste of ritual drummers. Regardless of which interpretation one prefers, it is indisputable that the name gestures to a low social caste status. Thus, as the legend builds, his social identity becomes crucial. He is of mixed parentage—his father is a brahmin and his mother a Dalit—and is abandoned at birth to be raised first by a weaver and then by an agriculturalist. He is the youngest of seven children, all of whom are similarly abandoned but transcend their circumstances to achieve fame of various sorts, some becoming great poets, while others become goddesses. He is itinerant, traveling to sacred mountains in the Tamil country, to the coastal city of Mylai, to Madurai, the center of Tamil learning. It is in Madurai that the famous test of the Kural occurs at the Sangam Academy of Poets, and thus humbled, each of the Sangam poets composes a verse in praise of Vaḷḷuvar's poem, cre-

* For a discussion of this vocabulary, see Zvelebil, *Tamil Literature*, 125n86, and for a discussion of the poet's Jain orientation/religious orientation more generally, see Shulman, *Tamil: A Biography*, 95.

ating the *Tiruvaḷḷuva Mālai.** He eventually returns to Mylai to live out his last days as a weaver. Curiously, Vaḷḷuvar's iconography, which emerges alongside the written versions of his story, belies this tale of an iconoclast, of a traveler, a weaver, or a drummer of lowly origins. Instead, he is depicted draped in the robes of an ascetic, with a flowing beard, clutching a palm-leaf manuscript in his left hand, while his right either grips a stylus or makes the gesture of wisdom. These images, some of which are consecrated, like at the Vaḷḷuvar temple in the city of Chennai, replicate the popular iconography of the wise sage and, in doing so, make the poet less ambiguous and more scrutable than he is.

The meaning of the Vaḷḷuvar legend and the history of the Tirukkural's commentaries have been masterfully explored by Stuart Blackburn and Norman Cutler, respectively.† They both observe that the Tirukkural has long served as a fulcrum in the debates about Tamil literature and, by extension, concerns about Tamil identity. As the intricacies of this complex social history are beyond the scope of this short piece, I will refrain from repeating their arguments. Suffice to say that each has shown how stories and commentaries reflect the political and social concerns of their period, even as they, like Vaḷḷuvar's iconography, narrow the possibilities presented by a nameless poet who could have been a Jain, a Hindu, an ascetic, a householder, a yogi, or a synthesis of all these identities. But leaving aside these important questions about authorship and meaning making, what kinds of answers could we find then if we shifted our focus to the text's implied audience?

---

* The story of the composition of the verses in praise of the Kural (i.e., the *Tiruvaḷḷuvar Mālai*) by the Sangam poets' collective is clearly apocryphal. The Sangam test is a powerful, recurring motif in several stories about similar kinds of poets, and it is used very effectively in the Vaḷḷuvar legend. For a thorough discussion of the Vaḷḷuvar legend, see Stuart Blackburn, "Corruption and Redemption: The Legend of Valluvar and Tamil Literary History," *Modern Asian Studies* 34, no. 2 (May 2000): 449–82.

† For a discussion of the long history of Tirukkural commentary, see Norman Cutler, "Interpreting Tirukkural: The Role of Commentary in the Creation of a Text," *Journal of the American Oriental Society* 112, no. 4 (October–December 1992): 549–66.

The Kural is divided into three unequal books (*pāl*), concerning three domains of life in the world—virtue (*aṟam*), wealth (*poruḷ*), and love (*iṉpam*). The middle book is its longest section, accounting for sixty-nine chapters (39–108), while the first is thirty-eight (1–38) and the last, a mere twenty-four (109–133). This uneven division might suggest something of where the text's emphasis lies, or conversely, where it sees the greatest need for the counsel it offers—in good governance and polity. A kingdom is only as virtuous and good as a king and his counsel, and thus, we have in Book 2, chapters on the Splendor of Kings (39), Good Rule (55), Harsh Rule (56), and an entire section on the Arms of Government (64–95). Curiously, it is in this subsection that we encounter two meditations on two kinds of women—the courtesan (911–920) and the wife (901–910). The advice to the men (but not the women, of course) is the same: be wary of them. A strong man, a *virtuous* man, is not beguiled by either wife or courtesan, and only the heedless fall prey to the charms of women. Two examples from Thomas Pruiksma's lovely translations will make the point:

On courtesans, the poet says:

915 The wise of good minds do not seek the thin pleasure
Of those whose goods are common

While he has this to say about a man who is thrall of his wife:

902 The wealth of one craving his wife without care
Brings shame on himself and all men

But perhaps most damning, and one that seems to give the game away, is this couplet:

909 For him who does only his wife's bidding—no virtue
No wealth no pleasure

Virtue, wealth, and pleasure *are* the building blocks and aims of a good life (the Sanskrit *puruṣārtha*), the fourth of which is release from the world. That the Kural so explicitly denies the possibility of the very aims and purpose of a good life to a man who listens to his wife not only affirms that such pursuits are only available to men (and indeed, men of a particular status) but warns of the dire consequences should a man not assert his dominance. Indeed, in this very section, we hear the flip side—

907 Modesty in a woman is far more glorious
Than servility in a man

In the world of the Kural, the primary audience is male, and the well-lived life he should aspire to includes a chaste wife and good sons. The man should aim for a female life-mate (51–60) who reveres no god but her husband (55), and that all is ashes if the wife lacks glory (52). In the section that follows on offspring (61–70), the praise of gender-neutral children, such as in this verse—

63 It is said one's children are one's wealth—their wealth
Comes from one's deeds

—gives way to an emphasis on sons as the bearers of one's future:

67 The good of father to son—to make him
Stand forth among men

69 A mother rejoices even more than at birth hearing
That her son commands wisdom

Unsurprisingly, there is nothing in the 1,330 couplets of the Tirukkural about daughters, the joy they bring, or that they too might command wisdom. So, despite its lofty and deserved status as an enduring book of wisdom, the Kural too is marked by the social conditions of its time, which define women primarily in relation to men, locates power in their chastity, and their worthiness as mothers to sons. While we have a smattering of female poets in the classical period (1–3 CE), and a female poet here and there until the twentieth century, the female perspective is largely absent from the Tamil literary corpus. In this, the Tamil canon is not dissimilar to other canons the world over. But I would argue that the Tirukkural does offer us possibility to read against the grain and to make a different kind of meaning; these can be found in its structure and in the third and final book on love (titled simply "Love" in Pruiksma's translation).

This last, and shortest, book contains some of the most poignant, evocative verses on erotic love in all its forms. Although clearly indebted to the Tamil classical literary tradition's exploration of interiority, the Tirukkural strips its predecessors' complicated, allusive imagery and provides in its place a distilled, dense accounting of this most fundamental of human relationships. Here too there is universalizing—a love that radiates from an ideal (heteronormative) couple within the poem to encompass anyone who has known it:

1166 Love is an ocean of bliss but the pain
It brings is greater

But there is particularity too, the *particular* love shared by a man and a woman, and remarkably, we hear the woman's voice. Her love is not different in texture or in intensity than the man's. She yearns for him as he does for her.

He says, on first seeing her:

1083 I did not know death but now I do—
Fierce feminine eyes

And she says when apart from him:

1152 His sight brought pleasure but fearing he'll go
His touch brings pain

Each is fiercely connected to the other, as though one body. So, he says:

1122 What connects body and breath—that
Connects me to her

And she reflects:

1185 Look there—he goes—look here—this pallor
Comes to my body

The description of love, by both the male and female personae in this section, is largely tropic: he is wounded by her eyes; she grows pale in his absence, and so on. Yet, unlike in the rest of the poem, which privileges male experience of the world, in the Book of Love, we find women both as objects and subjects. Even if this depiction is stylized and largely imagines women as passive (they are usually rooted in place, left to suffer a man's departure or his infidelity), and even if the role for women is narrowly circumscribed to the realm of the interior, of domesticity, I would suggest that the universalizing pull of many of these couplets affords the opportunity to transcend their tropic particularity. Who in the grand throes of love and filled with doubt at the beloved's attachment hasn't experienced a version of this woman's words?

1204 Am I there too in his heart—he
Is always in mine

The Book of Love offers rich possibilities for a recuperative reading practice. But what of the Tirukkural as a whole? Here, I would like to return to the text's structure. As mentioned above, the Kural is divided into three books, which are themselves divided into several discrete, thematic chapters. Each of these chapters has ten couplets. If we accept that the Kural is a unitary work, then the chapters and the books into which they are set build toward a conclusion.* For instance, centuries of commentators have accepted that the absence of a book on liberation (*vīṭu/mokṣa*) is because the pursuit of the first three aims—virtue, wealth, and love—guarantees the fourth.† In other words, liberation is to be found and achieved in a thoroughly well-lived, *complete* life. But beyond this overarching argument about the nature and purpose of life, there are micro-arguments too that exist within the text. Let us take, for instance, the Kural's opening sections, which proffer advice on a range of topics to a non-gendered audience. For example, the section "The Home Life" (41–50) says this:

42 To the impoverished the forsaken and the dead
The one at home is friend

* David Shulman argues against the unity of the Tirukkural, although he sees cohesion in the Book of Love. Shulman, *Tamil: A Biography*, 94–96.

† One might also theorize that dropping the fourth book might have been one way to appeal to a broad audience, to affirm the text's nonsectarian leanings. A book on liberation would have necessitated the articulation of a specific soteriology—Jain, Brahmanical-Hindu, Yogic, Buddhist—immediately narrowing its audience. That the Kural's premodern commentators represent a range of religious affiliations speaks to the capaciousness of the text, absent this fourth book.

And then this:

45 If a life at home has love and virtue—that
Is its root and flower

The aphorisms apply equally to men and women, perhaps even to the company of children and a wide extended family. But the very next section, "In Praise of One's Life Companion" (51–60), makes it clear that the text is primarily concerned with the home life of men, which is itself tied to women's chastity, fidelity, and devotion:

57 What safety is the safety of walls—the safety within
Keeps her safe

So, if we read the Kural as a unitary text, then the later chapters on children, courtesans, fidelity, and so on seem only to confirm that the Kural's universalist ethics are not intended for everyone. But what if this is not the only way to read the text? What if we see the text's structure as supple and flexible? And indeed, this is also how centuries of the Tirukkural's interlocutors have engaged with it, extracting verses here and there, citing them to make a point about generosity, virtue, goodness, governance, or hospitality. That is, the Tirukkural's couplets are both meant to exist as independent, context-free aphorisms as well as embedded within a much longer ethical, didactic argument. Thus, a verse like this—

431 Those free of anger pride and depravity
Attain wealth with glory

—can be placed on the walls of a public bus to be read and reflected on by any number of passengers, of any class, any caste, any gender. The individual couplets shine on their own, like unset gemstones, and as an elegantly crafted necklace, where each jewel contributes to the beauty of the whole. It is in the ability of the Tirukkural to straddle the general and the particular, for its wisdom to be rooted in Tamil conceptions of gender, hospitality, or generosity, yet inviting a reader to go beyond them, that has ensured its vibrant afterlife. Capacious and puzzling, the Tirukkural invites constant contemplation, both as a complete text of 1,330 couplets and as a collection of 1,330 aphorisms.

Over the past eighteen months, we have lived through a global pandemic that has confronted us all with the difficult questions of what it means to live well. We have asked ourselves how to live in physical isolation, what responsibilities we have to ourselves and to our kin, and to our communities. Across the world, many have faced the apathy and cruelty of governments and of a governance that has failed to ensure the well-being of citizens. Amidst the chaos, we have come to appreciate our interconnectedness, that the wellness of one requires the wellness of all. The Kural expresses this in an aphorism composed as if for our times:

950 Healer patient medicine preparer—these four
Together are medicine

But even as some in the world glimpse a life after the pandemic, we feel the blistering effects of catastrophic climate change bearing down on us. Here, in drought-stricken California, I read a verse such as this—

20 No being can be without water—nothing can flow
For anyone without rain

—and immediately recognize a fundamental but oft forgotten truth, that human flourishing hinges on ecological flourishing, a lesson the Tirukkural teaches, but with a light, allusive touch. I, like countless others before me, have found comfort and counsel in the verses of this marvelous text in these trying times. To live as the wise Kural advises us to—in a state of chronic, cultivated empathy and in service of others—is indeed to live right and to live well.

ARCHANA VENKATESAN

CHERISHING GUESTS

A Translator's Preface to Tiruvalluvar's Tirukkural

Twenty-two years ago, when I first lived in Madurai in the state of Tamil Nadu, I went to visit the home of a student at the college where I was teaching. Meenakshi Sundram lived on a narrow lane not far from the Meenakshi Temple in this venerable and beautiful South Indian city. His home was only a few rooms, but they filled with family, friends, and neighbors, all eager to greet the teacher from abroad who could somehow speak a little Tamil. Meenakshi's parents fed me a sumptuous feast, and at the end of the lovely and leisurely evening, they surprised me with a gift: two books of Tamil poetry. One was a collection by a contemporary poet; the other, a special edition of Tiruvalluvar's Tirukkural. Meenakshi's father pointed to the cover of the second, dust-jacketed book. "Everything you need to know is in here," he said. "There are chapters on every aspect of life. When you have learned Tamil fully, you must read this book well."

I had no idea at the time how my interest in the language was going to blossom. It would be years before I could delve fully into any kind of Tamil literature, let alone an ancient classic. But I did know something of the importance of the Tirukkural, one of the most celebrated books in Tamil's two millennia of literary history. I'd seen quotes from it posted overhead in the city buses and had heard my Tamil teacher, Dr. K. V. Ramakoti, refer to several of the book's memorable verses. And so, in 2003 and 2004, when I returned to India on a Fulbright grant, I spent the second half of my stay studying the Tirukkural with Dr. Ramakoti as a guest in his home, tying the work to what I'd learned from him about the literature that precedes it and how different poets understand and express the relationship between people and place. Each day we read another chapter from the book, exploring not only the poetry itself but all the major commentaries that have grown up around it. As part of the process, I also memorized a selection of more than half of its verses, a far cry from the tradition of learning the entire volume by heart but enough at least to start getting some of its rhythms into my body.

The Tirukkural, or more simply, the Kural, is indeed an extraordinary work. Scholars often date it between the third and fifth centuries CE, at the end of what is known as the Sangam period, a time of literary flourishing in Tamil Nadu. The name of the book combines the honorific prefix *tiru*—"eminent," "beautiful," "holy"—with the name of the Tamil verse form that Tiruvalluvar employs, the *kuṟaḷ veṇpā*. More than one translator has referred to the kural form as a couplet, but doing so risks a misunderstanding. While a kural does consist of two lines of poetry, they are not matched metrically, as a couplet by Shakespeare or Pope might be. The first line of a kural contains four feet (*cīr*, in Tamil), while the second contains a mere two and a half. In addition, a kural is not end-rhymed but rather follows a sophisticated and nuanced pattern of assonance and consonance that has characterized Tamil poetry from its beginnings. Within the rhythm of each line, key vowel sounds are expected to correspond with each other (assonance), and key consonants, at the beginnings of words as well as within them, are expected to match exactly (consonance). It is an exceedingly compact and demanding form. (During my Fulbright year, I learned to write Tamil kurals myself, composing a handful of verses each morning before breakfast and showing them to Dr. Ramakoti for correction and emendation. They were not great poetry, but writing them deepened my understanding of Tamil prosody considerably.)

Tiruvalluvar uses this form to elucidate what it means to live a good life. Each chapter of the Kural consists of ten kurals on a single theme, such as friendship, hospitality, or rain. These verses are both complete in themselves and part of a larger whole in which all the different verses complement, augment, and amplify each other. The book's 133 chapters, in turn, are arranged into sections that cover three of the four aims prescribed by Hindu tradition—virtue, wealth, and love. Most commentators claim, and I'm inclined to agree, that Tiruvalluvar leaves out the fourth aim—liberation from the cycle of birth and death—because if a person pursues the first three wholeheartedly, the fourth is a natural result.

The book thus covers a vast array of human knowledge, experience, and wisdom, offering an intricate interweaving of ethics and poetry, full of wordplay, sharp imagery, and rhythmic sophistication. Its scope is so sweeping that some scholars have argued that Tiruvalluvar isn't actually a person but rather an emblem for a collective persona whose poems have been gathered into one volume. Either way, however, it is the work itself that matters. In the years since my first entry into its pages, Dr. Ramakoti would sometimes remark to me, "Wouldn't it be good if someone did a proper literary translation of the Tirukkural, drawing on all the commentaries that we studied together?" I would always agree, but it never crossed my mind that this hypothetical someone might be me. Until unexpectedly, five years ago, it suddenly occurred to me to try.

When I told Dr. Ramakoti that I was starting to make a translation, he exclaimed, "Oh good, you finally got it." It may have been obvious to him all along, but I don't think I could have even entertained the thought until I felt my knowledge of Tamil was clear enough and my practice as a poet solid enough to do some kind of justice to the task. Which is perhaps why he never suggested it to me directly. He knew it had to occur to me in its own time.

One may well ask why a new translation is even needed. The Kural is by far the most translated book from Tamil literature, with over eighty translations into different world languages, some made directly and many more made by way of English, since English serves as a common language in both India and beyond. Many of these translations, however, are neither literary nor in print, and several are entirely unreadable. The best of them, that of P. S. Sundaram, captures Tiruvalluvar's brevity and playfulness but does little to suggest his patterns of consonance and assonance. Here, for instance, is how Sundaram renders a verse from chapter 11, "Gratitude":

103 Help given regardless of return
Is wider than the sea*

* Tiruvalluvar, *The Kural*, trans. P. S. Sundaram (New York: Penguin Books, 1991).

And here is a transliteration of this verse, with several elements of its patterns in bold:

103 payaṉ **tūkkār** seyta utavi **na**yaṉ **tūkki**ṉ
naṉmai kaṭaliṟ peritu

Very little of these patterns has made it into Sundaram's translation. My experience, however, suggests that more is possible. Even if one can't achieve exactly the same effect with the same means—the same exact sounds in the same exact order—one can try to achieve a similar effect with similar means. That, in any case, is what I've tried to do, while also trying to honor root meanings. In this verse, for instance, *tūkkār* means literally "those not weighing":

103 The **weight** of good done without **weighing** results—**gra**ce
Greater than oceans

Two other aspects of Tiruvalluvar's poetry have eluded previous translations: the dissimilar lengths of the lines in a kural and the absence of punctuation. (Tamil didn't have or need punctuation as we know it until the language encountered English.) Accordingly, I've tried to honor this dissymmetry in each verse and have also drawn on the example of the North American poet W. S. Merwin, who relinquished punctuation while writing his fifth book, *The Moving Target*. He felt, and I feel, that punctuation staples a poem to a page, pinning it within the rational protocol of written language and literal-minded prose. I want instead to evoke the oral and aural qualities of Tiruvalluvar's intelligence, which cannot be fully captured by mere rationality. He speaks to all of our senses with all of his. So although at times I use a dash to make the meaning clearer, as well as initial capitals to suggest the formality of the verse, I have strenuously avoided any other kind of punctuation. This is meant to encourage readers to read the poems out loud and to allow their breath and their ears to participate in the discovery of the verses' many patterns and meanings.

In some cases the dashes are also meant to suggest a form of expression in Tamil that doesn't have an exact equivalent in English. Many of Tiruvalluvar's statements equate one thing to another, as we might do in English with a form of the verb "to be." I might say, for instance, "My name is Thomas," and we'd understand that the verb "is" equates "my name" and "Thomas." In Tamil, however, one doesn't need a verb to make such a statement. One can simply place the two elements beside each other and their connection will be clearly understood. What looks literally like "My name Thomas" means in fact "My name is Thomas." But in English, if we write "My name Thomas," we're not really writing in English. Unless, that is, we say the statement out loud and add a pause of some significance between "name" and the name itself: "My name—Thomas." Now we have something that brings the two forms of expression a bit closer. And notice that this not only returns us to language as it's spoken but to the drama that such a pause out loud can convey.

I have thus used dashes to indicate places where a pause may help to bring the poem off the page. Here's an example from chapter 2, "The Glory of Rain":

> *15* That which ruins and raises up
> The ruined—rain

One could, of course, translate the dash here as "is," but I feel that it's closer to the spirit and energy of the original to convey that meaning with a more meaningful silence. Doing so also keeps the poem more open to possibility and to different interpretations, as all good poems tend to do. Throughout this translation, if a verse does not seem at first to make sense to you, speak it out loud and you may find it revealing its patterns of meaning to your ear. Poetry begins in the ear of the heart, which we can learn to hear through the ear of our body.

In order to interweave some of the contexts in which these verses find meaning, I have included some brief notes to explain key cultural and literary ideas. These notes, taken together, form a kind of commentary, one that corresponds to what is known in Tamil as "a commentary of notes." I first encountered this kind of commentary reading another Tamil classic, Iḷaṅkō Aṭikaḷ's *Cilappatikāram* (*The Tale of an Anklet*), and appreciate the way it gives just enough background for readers to enter the writing more fully without taking over the process entirely. In that spirit, I've given notes to amplify the connotations of words and to offer further insight into the verses themselves, especially about what goes on behind the scenes of the translation. For instance, although one might wish to translate key words from the Tamil in the same way throughout the book, this isn't always possible or even desirable, given how meanings can shift in different contexts. Hence, the notes clarify where different words in English may be translating the same word in Tamil, or where the same word in English may be rendering, at different times, different words in the original.

The notes also serve another purpose. Present-day readers of the Kural in Tamil almost never read the work without a commentary of some kind. In making this translation, I have referred to the oldest traditional commentaries available, written between the eleventh and fourteenth centuries. Where it has seemed helpful to do so, I have included certain observations from the last and most authoritative of these commentators, Parimēlaḻakar, as well as from the earliest and in some ways my favorite, Maṇakkuṭavar. In this way I mean to suggest how interpretive frameworks such as theirs are part of the experience of reading Tiruvalluvar in Tamil. If at times I offer a pair of conflicting interpretations, I don't do so to say that these are the only ones possible but rather to suggest there may be still others.

Two last textual notes: Most of the time, in writing Tamil words in English, I have used the transliteration system of the *Tamil Lexicon*, published by the University of Madras. However, though such systems can be useful for scholars, the diacritical marks they include can also serve inadvertently to mystify a language and hide it behind a screen of scholarly expertise. So, in some cases, where it feels right to do so, I have transliterated words according to my ear instead, so that a reader can hear what I'm talking about without recourse to a system that requires some initiation to make sense of. I have also omitted the diacritics on Tamil (Tamiḻ), Tirukkural (Tirukkuṟaḷ), and Tiruvalluvar (Tiruvaḷḷuvar), in honor of how these names have become naturalized in English.

Finally, I have followed the practice of most Tamil editions of the Kural and ordered the verses in each chapter according to Parimēlaḻakar's commentary. (Other commentators, such as Maṇakkuṭavar, sometimes order the verses differently.) I have also included a number of Parimēlaḻakar's insights about how various chapters form larger groupings, and how these groupings in turn help us in reading the poems. But I would encourage the reader to keep returning to the verses themselves and to remain open to one's own discoveries. The Kural is not simply a book to read but a work to engage and converse with. That is how its verses come most alive, able to startle and illuminate.

Each reader and listener will find verses that speak directly to their own experience. Here are three that I love and that have helped me become more fully who I am. In chapter 8, "Having Love," Tiruvalluvar speaks of the kind of love that brings families and friends together. The first verse of its ten has helped me remain open to both the sorrow and the beauty of life's comings and goings:

> *71* Is there a latch for love—the fullness of one's heart
> Shows in the tears that well

When I have sorrowed in parting, I have found consolation in Tiruvalluvar's reminder that this sorrow grows from fullness and from daring to say yes to love in the first place.

Another verse, from chapter 11, "Gratitude," has tempered my tendency to dwell on what feels wrong in the past:

> *108* Forgetting good done is not good—forgetting at once
> What is not good—good

It may seem strange here that Tiruvalluvar would counsel forgetting, especially when he speaks elsewhere of power and justice. But what I've taken from this verse is that the longer I nurse a sense of being wronged, the less energy I have to remember and enact goodness. Goodness grows from goodness remembered.

And in the first kural of chapter 9, "Hospitality," Tiruvalluvar encapsulates the point of having and upholding the householder's life:

> *81* The life of cherishing and being at home—for cherishing guests
> With generosity

I have known this generosity in Tamil Nadu beyond anything I could ever have asked for—from students, from friends, from people who have made me part of their family. And so I dedicate this translation to all the people of Tamil Nadu who have welcomed me into their homes, and especially to the late Dr. K. V. Ramakoti, who taught me far more than just language. He read every line of this translation, pushing me to ever greater fidelity to the Tamil and ever greater intensity in the English. I was able to spend the summer of 2017 tossing these verses back and forth with him in his home and will never forget the gift of that summer, nor the gift of all the time he spent offering what he knows. It is because of him that I am finally able to respond fully to the gift that Meenakshi Sundram and his family gave to me all those years ago.

THE KURAL

PART ONE

VIRTUE

I INTRODUCTION

1. IN PRAISE OF GOD

1 All speech starts from ah—as the world
Starts from God

2 Without touching the feet of one who is truth
What good is study

3 At the feet of a mind in flower a person
Lives long upon earth

4 At the feet of a mind beyond like and dislike a person
Knows no suffering

5 The two deeds that bring darkness bring nothing to those
Singing the true glory of God

6 A person lives long on the truthful path
Of those free of all five senses

7 Except at the feet of one without peer—hard
To escape the heart's suffering

8 Except at the feet of an ocean of compassion—hard
To cross the other two

9 Like senses without sense—the head that won't bow
To those embodying all virtue

10 A swimmer cannot swim the sea of birth
Without touching the feet of God

2. THE GLORY OF RAIN

11 Because rain gives us the world—fitting to know it
As ambrosia

12 Making food fit for feeding and itself
Food that feeds—rain

13 If skies fail to rain hunger racks the wide earth
Surrounded on all sides by seas

14 The plowmen won't plow if the wealth
Of storm clouds has withered

15 That which ruins and raises up
The ruined—rain

16 If clouds do not let their drops fall—hard to see even
One tip of green grass

17 If clouds of lightning do not gather and give
Even the great seas will shrink

18 For beings in heaven no festivals no prayers
If the heavens dry up below

19 No generosity or austerity can grace this great world
If the skies grant nothing above

20 No being can be without water—nothing can flow
For anyone without rain

3. THE GREATNESS OF LETTING GO

21 Good books agree—the great let go in that way
Which is theirs

22 Letting go is how great—great as how many
Have died on earth

23 Knowing the two and choosing to let go—no
Greater glory in this world

24 He who leads the five with the prod of solidity—
A seed in the best of all lands

25 To the power that commands all five Indra himself
Lord of gods bears witness

26 The great do the impossible—the small do
What everyone can

27 The world is theirs who fathom all five—
Sight sound touch taste smell

28 The secret spoken by those of true words
Shows their greatness on earth

29 From those who have climbed character—hard to stand even
One moment of rage

30 Those who let go embody grace—they show
Compassion to all

4. THE IMPERATIVE OF RIGHT ACTION

31 It grants eternity and also grants wealth—what gains
A life more than doing right

32 Nothing gains more than virtue—nothing destroys more
Than forgetting it

33 As best as one can do right without ceasing
Everywhere that right can be done

34 Right action is purity of heart-and-mind—all else
Nothing but noise

35 Envy desire anger bitter words—right action
Is freedom from all four

36 Do right without waiting—at death it remains
Beside one undying

37 No need to speak of virtue—look who is borne
And who bears the palanquin

38 It closes the way back like a weir—enacting what's good
Without wasting one day

39 Right action brings happiness—all else
Oblivion and pain

40 Action that fits is virtue—action
That doesn't is vice

II HOUSEHOLDING

5. THE HOME LIFE

41 One at home stands in goodness—foundation
Of the three other stations

42 To the impoverished the forsaken and the dead
The one at home is friend

43 Nothing is higher than honoring the five realms—
Spirits gods guests relations self

44 A life that shares food and fears wrong—way
Without end in the world

45 If a life at home has love and virtue—that
Is its root and flower

46 If one does right living at home—what good is
Doing anything elsewhere

47 One true to the life at home stands above
All others who strive

48 The home life that guides others—greater
Than greatest austerity

49 The life at home is itself right action—and good
When free of all blame

50 Those on earth thriving in the life at home—held
Among gods in heaven

6. IN PRAISE OF ONE'S LIFE COMPANION

51 She whose greatness suits home and her husband's
Abundance alike—that is a life companion

52 If a wife lacks a wife's glory even with all other glories
The home life has none

53 What's lacking if a wife is great—what's not
If a wife is not

54 What is greater than a wife if she bears
The great strength of fidelity

55 She who rises revering no god but her husband
Says rain and the rain pours down

56 A true wife—one without weakness who cares for herself
Her husband and the power of words

57 What safety is the safety of walls—the safety within
Keeps her safe

58 If she gains him that gained her a wife gains
The greatness of heaven

59 He cannot tread before scorn like a lion—he whose wife
Does not sparkle with praise

60 A wife with glory is grace—and bearing
Good children its jewel

7. HAVING CHILDREN

61 Of all we may have we know nothing higher than having
Children with knowledge

62 Untouched by wrong in all seven lives—those
Whose children shun evil

63 It is said one's children are one's wealth—their wealth
Comes from one's deeds

64 Sweeter than ambrosia by far—the food the tiny hands
Of one's children have scattered

65 The touch of one's children—pleasure to the body—their words—
Pleasure to the ear

66 Those who don't hear the babble of their children
Call the flute and the lyre sweet

67 The good of father to son—to make him
Stand forth among men

68 Children whose knowledge exceeds one's own
Delight all lives on earth

69 A mother rejoices even more than at birth hearing
That her son commands wisdom

70 The aid of son to father—to hear people say
What did he do to have him

8. HAVING LOVE

71 Is there a latch for love—the fullness of one's heart
Shows in the tears that well

72 Everything belongs to the loveless—for the loving
Bones too belong to others

73 They call it the gift of love—the union
Of breath and bone

74 Love yields affection and that yields the boundless
Glory of friendship

75 They call it the fruit of loving—the glory awaiting
Those joyful on earth

76 It serves only virtue say those who don't know—but love
Is friend to wrong too

77 Like sun on a body writhing without bones
Virtue scorches the loveless

78 Like a withered tree in the desert sprouting leaves—living
With no love in one's heart

79 If a heart lacks the eye of love—what good
Is the eye of a body

80 Life endures by the ways of love—without it a body
Is but skin and bones

9. HOSPITALITY

81 The life of cherishing and being at home—for cherishing guests
With generosity

82 With a guest at the door it is not worth eating
Even the nectar of the gods

83 The life that cherishes strangers each day
Never falls upon ruin

84 Prosperity lives joyfully in the home that cherishes
Each good guest with a smile

85 He who partakes with his guests—need he ever
Plant seeds in the ground

86 Feeding the guests going and awaiting the guests coming—
Guests to the gods above

87 We cannot foretell the good of offering—it rests
On the nature of each guest

88 Those who don't dare to cherish their guests lament
The loss of their labors

89 Want in plenty is what fools possess who foolishly
Fail to cherish guests

90 Anicham flowers wilt when smelt—a guest wilts
When a face turns sour

10. SWEET SPEECH

91 Sweet speech—words mingled with love free of guile
Spoken by those who know truth

92 Speaking sweet words with a smile—better
Than giving with joy

93 Facing gently looking kindly speaking sweetly
With one's heart—that is right action

94 They do not know the hardship of hunger—those
Who speak sweetly with all

95 Humility and sweet speech adorn one in beauty—
All else does not

96 Good grows and wrong wanes if one who loves goodness
Speaks sweetly

97 They grant greatness and virtue—words that grant goodness
Without ceasing to be sweet

98 Sweet words without smallness bring happiness
Here and hereafter

99 Sweet words bring sweetness—seeing this why
Does anyone speak harshly

100 Speaking without sweetness sweet words within—like finding
Ripe fruit and eating sour

11. GRATITUDE

101 Hard even for heaven and earth to match—help given
Without help gained

102 Even if small help given in time—far
Far larger than the world

103 The weight of good done without weighing results—grace
Greater than oceans

104 Seen as a tree by those who can see—good done
The size of a seed

105 Help does not measure help—the heart of the helped
Measures help

106 Forget no bond with the blameless—renounce no friend
Who held through hard times

107 Remembered for all seven births—the friendship
That ends affliction

108 Forgetting good done is not good—forgetting at once
What is not good—good

109 Remembering one good that was done the worst
Of wrongs disappears

110 Kill goodness—redemption remains—kill gratitude—
Redemption is gone

12. FAIRNESS

111 Fairness alone is goodness—if one attains
Fairness with all

112 A fair man's wealth never falters—and offers
Protection to his progeny

113 Renounce at once wealth gained without fairness
Even if it brings only good

114 In seeing his children we know
If a man is fair

115 Rising and falling have never not been—an unbiased heart
Adorns wisdom

116 Know this—if I do wrong my heart failing
At fairness I'm ruined

117 The decline of one balanced in goodness—the wise
Do not deem it as ruin

118 Like a balance that weighs truly an impartial mind
Adorns the wise

119 Fairness means speech without bias—when bias
Is absent within

120 Good business for those who do business—caring
For others' goods as one's own

13. SELF-CONTROL

121 Self-control sets one among gods—its lack
Sets one in darkness

122 Safeguard composure like truth—no treasure
Is greater for the living

123 On the path of wisdom achieving control
Achieves glory and renown

124 Steady in one's state staying composed one stands
Taller than a mountain

125 Humility is good for all—and great wealth
For the wealthy

126 He who contains all five like a tortoise—safe
Through all seven lives

127 Guard one's tongue if nothing else—unguarded
One suffers how words slip

128 Good ceases to be good if one harms
Even once with harsh words

129 A wound left by fire heals within—
Not the scar left by words

130 Virtue awaits those who check anger learn deeply
And remain composed

14. THE POSSESSION OF CONDUCT

131 Conduct gives birth to greatness—guard conduct
More even than life

132 Guard conduct with unceasing care—one finds
No better companion

133 Conduct itself is nobility—a person
Falls low by losing it

134 A mantra may be relearned—a Brahmin destroying conduct
Destroys his birth

135 One has no glory with ill conduct—as one has
No bounty with jealousy

136 Knowing the anguish of its loss the strong
Hold firmly to conduct

137 The presence of conduct brings glory—its absence
Damnation beyond measure

138 Good conduct is seed to virtue—bad conduct yields
Sorrow without end

139 For those who have conduct wrong words do not slip
From one's lips

140 Those who can't flow with the world—even if learned
They know nothing

15. FIDELITY

141 The folly of wanting another man's wife—not found
In those who know virtue

142 Of those outside virtue no fool is greater than the one
Outside another's door

143 They are more than dead—those wronging
A trusting man's wife

144 The heedless man who enters another man's house—
However great what good is he

145 Taking a man's wife thinking it easy gains shame
That won't ever die

146 Enmity offense fear damnation—the man taking another's wife
Has these forever

147 A man embodies virtue not wanting the virtue
Of another man's wife

148 Not only virtue but fullness of conduct—the fortitude
That won't seek another's wife

149 Who attains glory on this earth of fierce waters—he
Who won't taste the arms of another's

150 Even doing evil and living without virtue a man does right
Not seeking the virtue of another man's wife

16. FORBEARANCE

151 Like earth that bears digging those who bear scorn
Stand highest

152 To bear transgression is always good—to forget it
Better than good

153 Want in want—turning away guests—strength in strength—
Bearing fools

154 If one seeks excellence without end protect
And practice forbearance

155 Those who hit back—held as nothing—those who forbear—
Cherished like gold

156 For those who hit back—one day of pleasure—for those who bear—
A life of renown

157 Better to suffer wrong than to wrong
Others who wrong you

158 To overpower arrogant insolence practice
Inborn patience

159 Purer than saints—those who endure
Vicious mouths

160 Those who endure without eating are great—after those
Who endure harsh words

17. FREEDOM FROM ENVY

161 Take as the way of virtue—freedom
From envy in one's heart

162 Gain that cannot be equaled—freedom
From envy from any

163 The envious who won't honor it in others
Forfeit the fruit of virtue

164 Knowing the misery of misconduct one
Does no wrong out of envy

165 It alone is enough—even without enemies envy
Eviscerates the envious

166 They perish without food without clothing—the family
Of one jealous of giving

167 Fortune fed up with the envious consigns them
To her wayward sister

168 Envy is a fiend—it ravages wealth and flings us
Into the fire

169 Ponder whether the jealous heart has riches
And the good one ruin

170 None grow great through envy—none
Without it lack plenty

18. FREEDOM FROM GREED

171 He without fairness who covets good things falters
And shatters his family

172 They do not do wrong wishing for gain—those
Who shrink from bias

173 They do not do wrong coveting small pleasures—those
Who seek another pleasure

174 They do not covet thinking they are poor—those who command
Their senses and see

175 What good is great learning if the learned
Do wrong out of greed

176 The thought of wrong ruins him—the seeker of grace
Coveting others' things

177 They yield no greatness—shun riches
Born out of greed

178 What keeps abundance abundant—not craving
What other hands hold

179 Seeing their virtue fortune embraces
Those free of all greed

180 Thoughtless greed brings ruin—the pride
Of not needing brings triumph

19. FREEDOM FROM BACKBITING

181 Even speaking no goodness and doing evil—biting
No backs is sweetness

182 Worse than cursing good and doing evil—biting another's back
While smiling to their face

183 In place of living falsely biting backs—dying
Confers the wealth of virtue

184 Even speaking evil before others speak nothing
Behind them forgetting what follows

185 Vile and backbiting words betray hearts
That speak no virtue

186 He who proclaims the faults of others will have
His best faults proclaimed

187 They divide old friends with their words—those
Who can't speak joyfully and make friends

188 Those who broadcast the faults of their friends—what
Won't they do to strangers

189 The weight of backbiting men—does the earth
Bear it for virtue

190 If one sees one's faults as one sees them in others
What harm can come to one's soul

20. FREEDOM FROM FRUITLESS SPEECH

191 Those who speak without fruit angering many—
Despised by all

192 Fruitless speech before many—worse
Than heartlessness to friends

193 Fruitless speech spoken without end
Tells the absence of goodness

194 Fruitless and denatured words in an assembly
Destroy goodness and grace

195 If the good speak without fruit all wealth
And glory leave them

196 He who celebrates words without fruit—not a son
But the husk of a man

197 The wise may speak without goodness but it is good
Never to speak without fruit

198 The wise who consider the highest fruit
Will not speak one fruitless word

199 Those who see truth with clear eyes never lapse
Into words without meaning

200 Speak speech that bears fruit—never speech
That bears nothing

21. FEAR OF WRONGDOING

201 The excellent fear it—the evil do not—the confusion
Of doing wrong

202 Wrong begets wrong—fear wrong
Beyond fire

203 Chief of all knowing—not wronging
Those who wrong us

204 Even when forgetful mean no harm—virtue means harm
To those who mean harm

205 Do no wrong thinking you have nothing—if you do
You will—again and again

206 If one wishes no misery inflict
No evil on others

207 One may escape any foe—but wrong
Relentless destroys in time

208 Like a shadow underfoot—the ruin
Of wrongdoers

209 If one loves oneself do not think
Even the least wrong

210 Know this—one knows no harm by doing
No wrong and not straying

22. KNOWING WHAT IS FITTING

211 Kindness seeks no return—what does the earth
Return to the rain

212 Wealth earned through effort—all for being generous
To those whom it fits

213 Nothing better to have here or in heaven than
Generosity that fits

214 They live who know kindness—all others are placed
Among the dead

215 A well of abundant water—the wealth of the wise
Who love the world

216 A tree bearing fruit at the heart of town—wealth
In the hands of good people

217 A tree granting remedies freely to all—wealth
In the hands of great people

218 Even in tight times they won't cease to be generous—those
Who embody true kindness

219 Lacking a way to do what is fitting—that
Is poverty to the good

220 If generosity yields ruin—ruin is worth having
Even by selling oneself

23. GIVING

221 Giving to those with nothing is giving—all else
Expects a return

222 Even leading to heaven taking is wrong—even leading to hell
Giving is good

223 Giving and not crying I have nothing—found
In those of good family

224 It is bitter to be begged—till the face
That begged turns sweet

225 Strength of the strong—strength over hunger—after those
Whose strength relieves hunger

226 Ending the ruinous hunger of the poor—a safe
That stores a man's wealth

227 The vicious disease that is hunger cannot touch
Those who share food

228 The callous who lose all that they keep—do they not know
The joy of giving

229 More bitter than begging—balancing books by
Eating alone

230 Nothing more bitter than death—but death is sweet
If one cannot give

24. RENOWN

231 Give freely and gain glory—nothing else
Gains a life more

232 The glory of those giving what's needed—those
Who speak speak only of this

233 Nothing but peerless and soaring renown endures
Undying in this world

234 When one gains lasting renown on earth the heavens
Cease praising the saints

235 Gain in loss—life in death—the discerning alone
Attain them

236 If you appear appear with renown—better not to appear
Than to appear without it

237 Those with no renown not blaming themselves—why
Do they blame them who scorn them

238 A stain on all people—living without
Leaving a name

239 Even the blameless abundance of earth dwindles
Beneath bodies without name

240 Who lives without name does not live—who lives
Without blame lives

III RENUNCIATION

25. COMPASSION

241 The wealth of compassion—wealth among wealth—the wealth
of things—
Found also among fools

242 On the path of goodness achieve compassion—it alone
Sees one to the end of every path

243 One who knows compassion does not enter
The darkness of hell

244 Those with compassion who cherish all lives
Face nothing their life will fear

245 The fertile and windswept world stands witness—those
With compassion do not suffer

246 They lose everything but disdain—those who discard
Compassion and do wrong

247 No heaven without compassion—as no earth
Without wealth

248 Lacking possessions one may yet flourish—lacking compassion
One lacks for all time

249 Like truth beheld without wisdom—virtue performed
Without compassion

250 Before those weaker—think of oneself
Before those stronger

26. REFUSING MEAT

251 He who eats flesh to fatten his own—how
Can he embody compassion

252 One commands no wealth without care—one commands
No compassion eating flesh

253 Like hearts that bear weapons no grace in minds
That relish others' flesh

254 Lack of compassion—killing not-killing—lack
Of virtue—eating what's killed

255 Life lies in not eating meat—eat and the jaws
Of hell clamp forever

256 None would seek to sell flesh if none sought
To eat by killing

257 If they knew it as the wound of another
People would not eat meat

258 They eat no flesh severed from life—those
Who have severed confusion

259 Not taking and eating one life—better than
A thousand offerings through fire

260 To those refusing to kill and eat meat all lives
Join hands in prayer

27. TAVAM

261 To bear suffering and to do no harm—that
Is the form of tavam

262 Those with tavam do tavam—those without it
Perform it in vain

263 Wanting to give to those who've let go
Did the others forget tavam

264 Enemies are ruined and friends raised up if the one
Who has tavam thinks it

265 It brings what is sought as sought—perform
Tavam in this life

266 Those who do tavam do their duty—caught in desire
Others cause their own ruin

267 In burning and burning gold brightens—enduring
Affliction brings light

268 Those whose lives aren't their own—revered
By all other lives

269 Those who attain tavam's power find freedom
From death at hand

270 Few do tavam—many do not—that is why
Many have nothing

28. UNWORTHY CONDUCT

271 At the hollow conduct of a dishonest heart
The five senses laugh within

272 Knowing wrong in one's heart what good
To tower to the sky

273 A show of command in one without it—a cow in tiger's skin
Munching crops

274 One who does wrong behind tavam—hunter
Behind bushes catching birds

275 The false conduct of him who says he needs nothing
Will make him cry out what have I done

276 None more cruel than those seeming to renounce
And living by falsehood

277 Some seeming as regal as a red rosary pea
Are as black at heart as its tip

278 Plunging into the waters of greatness many hide
False conduct in their hearts

279 The crooked lyre is sweet—the straight arrow harsh—one
Must know people by their deeds

280 If one keeps from what the wise call evil
No need to shave or grow tangles

29. FREEDOM FROM STEALING

281 One wanting no shame—watch that one's heart
Wishes to steal nothing

282 Even the thought is wrong—think not
To thieve another's things

283 Seeming to grow—gain gained by stealth
Declines utterly

284 Desire grown thick in thievery—misery
Without end in the end

285 For those set on things awaiting a lapse—no love
Set on compassion

286 They cannot fit what fits—those with desire
Grown thick in thievery

287 The darkness of stealing—unknown to those knowing
The strength of grace

288 Like good in a heart that loves grace—deception
In a heart that loves theft

289 They err and perish—those who know nothing
But thieving

290 Heaven never shuns those who don't steal—life
Always shuns those who do

30. TRUTH

291 What do we call truth—speech
Free of all evil

292 If falsehood begets immaculate good it too
Belongs with truth

293 Speak nothing the heart knows to be false—once spoken
The heart scorches oneself

294 One lives in all wise hearts if one lives
Without lies in one's heart

295 One stands above generosity and tavam when
One speaks truth with one's heart

296 It bestows all virtue without effort—nothing
Brings glory like not lying

297 Not doing and not doing all other good is yet good
If one masters not lying and not lying

298 Purity without comes by water—purity within
Comes by being true

299 For the wise all lamps are not lamps—only the lamp
Of not lying is lamp

300 In all that we see to be true nothing
Is truer than truth

31. FREEDOM FROM ANGER

301 They guard who guard where anger has sway—where not
Why guard or not guard

302 Anger is bad where it has no sway—where it has sway
Nothing is worse

303 Bear anger toward none—anger gives birth
To evil

304 Anger kills joy and laughter—is any
Enemy greater

305 To guard oneself guard against anger—unguarded
Anger destroys one

306 The fire of rage that kills all it touches burns
The raft of one's teachers

307 As surely as the earth to the hand that hits it—the ruin
Of those who take rage as power

308 Even when scorched by tongues of fire it is good
To forgo anger

309 All one conceives comes into being if one bears
No anger within

310 They are dead whose anger hasn't died—they are saints
Who sail beyond anger

32. DOING NO HARM

311 Precept of the flawless—not harming others
Even for wealth that brings glory

312 Precept of the flawless—not striking even them
Who struck them in fury

313 To harm one who harmed one for nothing brings hardship
Without hope of release

314 To punish wrongdoers ashame them with goodness
And release them

315 What good is knowledge if one doesn't see the suffering
Of another as one's own

316 What one has recognized to be harm
One must not do to another

317 Highest of all—intending no evil toward anyone
Anyway anywhere

318 Why would one harm the lives of others knowing
What harms one's life

319 Harm done to others before noon returns
Of its own by nightfall

320 Pain comes to those who pain others—those seeking
No pain pain none

33. FREEDOM FROM KILLING

321 Right action is not killing—killing
Brings all other wrongs

322 Of all that authors have gathered together—to share food
And cherish life stands highest

323 Foremost of virtues—not killing—close
Behind it—not lying

324 What is a good way—that which upholds
Killing nothing

325 Those who dread bloodshed and practice not killing—highest
Of those who dread stasis and let go

326 Life-ending death does not touch their days—those whose conduct
Does not touch killing

327 Take not the sweet life of another—even
If it takes one's life

328 Even if great and gained by virtue wealth gained by killing
Does not suit the wise

329 Those who kill are wretched—know hearts
That know what is base

330 Those living in misery and ill in body—they
Took lives from bodies

34. IMPERMANENCE

331 The basest and least of all sense—seeing what won't last
As what lasts

332 Great wealth arrives like a crowd to a show—and goes
As the crowd itself goes

333 Wealth by nature does not endure—when gained
Do what endures

334 What appears as a day—a blade
Flaying life if one sees

335 Before the stiff tongue and final gasp—take up
The good to be done

336 Here yesterday gone today—that
Is the glory of this world

337 They think millions on millions of thoughts—those who
Do not know they will live one moment

338 Like the bird departing its shell—the bond
Between life and body

339 Death is like sleeping—birth
Like waking from sleep

340 For the life sheltered in a body—is there no
Home that lasts

35. RENUNCIATION

341 One who lets go of any thing and any thing is free
Of the pain of that thing and that thing

342 Renounce in time if you seek—after you renounce
All that delights is here

343 Seek to subdue the senses—seek to release
All you seek through the senses

344 To hold nothing is the nature of tavam—holding
Prevents and confuses

345 Why have other bonds—to sever from birth
The body is more than enough

346 Who severs the pride of me and mine enters
The world beyond gods

347 Those who seize seizing without ceasing—seized
By trouble without ceasing

348 Those releasing completely touch heaven—all others
Fall into snares

349 Severing seizing severs rebirth—otherwise
Nothing can rest

350 Hold to the hold of one who holds nothing—to hold nothing
Hold to that hold

36. KNOWING WHAT IS REAL

351 Delusion that takes what is not real for the real
Leads to a birth without light

352 For those who depart from delusion—darkness
Departs—glory arrives

353 For those who see truth—leaving delusion—heaven
Is closer than earth

354 For those who cannot sense truth
The senses yield nothing

355 Whatever thing whatever kind—perceiving
Its truth is knowledge

356 Those who study and see truth here—reach
The path beyond here

357 If a mind perceive and penetrate truth—no need
To think of rebirth

358 Quelling birth's folly by seeing truth's splendor—
That is knowledge

359 If one severs all bonds knowing what bears one
The suffering that binds unbinds

360 Confusion anger craving—as their names disappear
Affliction disappears

37. SEVERING FROM DESIRE

361 The seed of incessant birth for all lives
At all times—desire

362 Desire no birth when desiring—it comes
Desiring no desire

363 Here no greater wealth than freedom from desire—nor anything
There to equal it

364 Purity is absence of desire—it comes
By seeking what is true

365 Those beyond desire are beyond—the rest
Only seem to be beyond

366 Desire itself betrays—fearing desire
Itself is virtue

367 Undying deeds happen as hoped if one severs
Desire completely

368 Those without desire do not suffer—those with it
Suffer without ceasing

369 If one ends desire—misery of miseries—even on earth
Unending joy

370 Releasing insatiable desire one finds in that moment
Glory that never ends

IV FATE

38. FATE

371 Fate that bears wealth bears energy—fate
That takes bears debility

372 Fate that ruins brings folly—fate that creates
Broadens knowledge

373 Even studying deep books—one's
Innate knowledge prevails

374 One thing to gain wealth—another to gain wisdom—
The nature of the world is two

375 When gaining all bad becomes good—when losing
All good becomes bad

376 However cast off what is fated won't go—however
Secured what is not won't stay

377 Unless fate decrees it one doesn't enjoy
Even many millions amassed

378 Those without would go without if only the suffering
Alloted them would pass

379 Why do they howl when things turn sour—those
Who call it good when things turn good

380 It exceeds every evasion—what
Is more powerful than fate

PART TWO

WEALTH

I SOVEREIGNTY

39. THE SPLENDOR OF KINGS

381 Castle kingdom force abundance advisors friends—the one
With these six stands highest

382 Generosity fearlessness knowledge energy—the nature of a king
Is these four in fullness

383 Tireless learned bold—one ruling a land
Must be these without ceasing

384 Unerring in virtue unyielding to evil unerring
In honor—that is a king

385 Strength that makes and earns and saves and assigns
What is saved—that is a king

386 Praised by the land—the king easy to approach
Free of all harsh words

387 The world abides in the word of one who cares
And gives with kind words

388 Counted a god among men—the king who protects
And carries out justice

389 The world abides beneath his umbrella—the king
Who bears bitter words

390 Generosity justice kindness vigilance—one with these four
A light for all kings

40. LEARNING

391 Faultlessly study what is to be studied—then fit
All that you've studied

392 The two called numbers and letters—eyes
For lives with life

393 The learned have eyes—the unlearned
Two wounds in their face

394 The work of the wise—delight on meeting
And feeling on leaving

395 Like the poor before the rich the learned bow low—those
Who won't learn are least

396 To the depth a person digs a well fills—to the depth
A person learns a mind deepens

397 It makes all places one's home and country—why wouldn't
A man learn till he dies

398 The learning one learns in one life—safeguard
Through all seven lives

399 When the world takes delight in what delights the learned
The learned grow in their love

400 Learning is sacred unperishing prosperity—all
Other wealth is not wealth

41. LACK OF LEARNING

401 Addressing the wise without knowing books—like playing
At chess with no board

402 Like a woman without breasts loving womanhood—a man
Without learning loving words

403 If they keep quiet before the learned even those
Without learning are great

404 Even if the unlearned shine for a moment
The wise do not call it wisdom

405 As the learned engage him the pride of a man
Without learning falls

406 Like salt-ridden soil that yields nothing—the unlearned
Exist—nothing more

407 An excellent doll made of mud—the beauty of a man
With no great knowledge

408 More bitter than the good meeting poverty—those
Without learning meeting wealth

409 Even if born high the unlearned cannot reach the greatness
Of the learned born low

410 As animals to men—men to those learned in books
That give light

42. LISTENING

411 Riches of the ear—riches among riches—highest
Of all other riches

412 When the ear lacks food feed a little
To the belly

413 Those on earth fed through their ear—like gods
Fed through their fire

414 Even if one lacks learning listen—it holds one up
When weary

415 Words given voice by the virtuous—staff
To keep one from slipping

416 Listen to what is good however little—that little
Can grant great renown

417 Those who listen deeply do not speak stupidities
Even by mistake

418 If the art of listening hasn't entered them—even when hearing
Ears do not hear

419 Unless one has heard the wise fully—hard
For a mouth to be humble

420 The wretched who savor mouths and not ears—
What difference if they live or die

43. THE POSSESSION OF KNOWLEDGE

421 Knowledge—tool that guards against ruin
And fortress that falls to no enemy

422 Knowledge keeps the mind steady and leads
From evil to goodness

423 Whatever one hears from whoever's mouth—discerning
Its truth is knowledge

424 Delivering the complex simply and discerning
What others say—that is knowledge

425 Befriending the wise is brilliance—and not blooming
And then drooping is wisdom

426 Moving with the great however the great move—
That is knowledge

427 Those who have knowledge foresee—those
Who do not do not

428 The work of knowing is fearing what's fearful—not fearing
What's fearful is folly

429 No sorrow can come to shake them—the wise
Who watch for what comes

430 Those with knowledge have all—those without it
Having all have nothing

44. ELIMINATION OF FAULTS

431 Those free of anger pride and depravity
Attain wealth with glory

432 Avarice arrogance exuberance without greatness—these
Are calamities for a king

433 For those who shun vice even one seed
Of wrong is a tree

434 Faults are foes that bring ruin—guard as treasure
Freedom from faults

435 The life of a king who won't guard beforehand
Falls like a haystack before fire

436 Discarding his faults and discerning those in others
What fault can any king have

437 The wealth of misers who won't do their duty
Withers declines and rots

438 Avarice that grips from within—vice
Unlike any other

439 Never acclaim oneself—nor desire
What doesn't produce good

440 If one loves what one loves in secret—the designs
Of foes fall to pieces

45. GAINING THE HELP OF THE GREAT

441 Those mature in knowledge and virtue—study
And gain their friendship

442 Befriend and cherish those able to end
And avert suffering

443 Rarest of rarities—cherishing the great
As one's own

444 Moving with those greater as one's own—highest
Of all great strengths

445 Counselors are eyes—a king must consider
And choose well

446 To one strong in right company and conduct
Enemies can do nothing

447 Who can ruin the king who rules counsel
Prepared to thunder

448 An unguarded king without counsel that thunders falls
Even without enemies

449 No profit without principal—nor permanence
Without pillars of support

450 Renouncing wise friends—ten times worse
Than earning foes

46. FREEDOM FROM SMALLNESS

451 Greatness fears smallness of company—the small
Consider it great company

452 The nature of earth alters water—the nature
Of company alters what we know

453 One's mind yields knowledge—one's company
Tells who one is

454 Knowledge appears of the mind but comes
Of the company we keep

455 Purity of mind and deed—both rest
On purity of company

456 Purity of mind bestows goodness—purity of company—
Nothing that fails

457 Virtuous minds bring wealth to all life—virtuous company—
All glory

458 Even for the wise with virtuous minds
Virtuous company is safety

459 A virtuous mind yields a good birth—and virtuous company
Protects it

460 No greater aid than good company—no
Greater torment than bad

47. CLARITY BEFORE ACTION

461 Consider what is spent what made and what gained—
Then act

462 No deed is impossible for those with clear counsel
Who then think choose and act

463 Deeds that deplete possibility for gain—the wise
Do not even begin them

464 Those that dread the error of dishonor
Begin nothing without clarity

465 How to plant your own patch of enemies—rise up
Without knowing what's what

466 Doing what is unworthy ruins—not doing
What is worthy also ruins

467 Ponder and proceed—proceeding and then saying
We'll ponder is folly

468 Without right effort all effort miscarries
Even with many who care

469 Enacted without knowing the character of all actors
Even right action contains error

470 The world won't credit what doesn't credit a king—think
And act beyond reproach

48. KNOWING STRENGTH

471 Assess a deed's power one's power opponents' power and the power
Of one's friends—then act

472 For those who stand firm in knowledge and possibility
No deed is undoable

473 Many have fallen midway—moving to move
Not knowing their strength

474 Failing to fit others ignoring his limits and flaunting
Himself a king falls quickly

475 Even the axle of a cart of feathers breaks
If heaped with too many

476 If one at the end of a branch keeps climbing
His life is over

477 Give rightly knowing one's limits—that is how
One honors and guards wealth

478 No harm when earning recedes if spending
Does not exceed it

479 A life that won't live within limits appears full
Then falls completely

480 Generosity that doesn't know what one has
Destroys what one has

49. KNOWING TIME

481 During the day the crow conquers the owl—kings
That conquer foes need time

482 Conduct that meets time—rope
That holds wealth together

483 With right means and right time is anything
Impossible

484 Seeking the time and place one seeking
The world can have it

485 They seek the right time unperturbed—those
Who seek the world

486 Like a ram retreating to attack—the restraint
Of a king with strength

487 Brilliance without rushing holds anger
Within—biding time

488 Bow before enemies till seeing their end—then—
See their heads low

489 When the rare moment arrives do what is rare
Without waiting

490 Wait like the crane that waits—and strike like the crane
When right

50. KNOWING PLACE

491 Till seeing where something may be routed
Scorn none—begin nothing

492 Even to the fierce able to face foes a fortress
Confers many gains

493 Knowing the place—protecting among opponents—
Even the powerless overpower

494 If friends act in force knowing the place
Opponents lose heart opposing

495 In deep waters a crocodile conquers—beyond them
Others conquer it

496 A strong-wheeled chariot cannot cross seas—nor a
Sea-crossing ship cross land

497 If one omits nothing and acts with the place
Courage alone will serve

498 If a leader of large armies enters a small place
His greatness crumbles

499 Hard to take people rooted in their land even if
They lack force and fortress

500 The elephant that has faced many foes without fear—defeated
In mire by a fox

51. KNOWING AND TRUSTING

501 Virtue wealth pleasure awe—discerning these four
In depth a king chooses

502 Born well free of faults unwilling to risk shame—
That's where trust belongs

503 Rare to find one free of all ignorance even
With rare learning and faultless

504 Know character know faults know which is greater—then
Take what is greatest

505 One's deeds alone—touchstone of greatness
Or smallness

506 Trust no one without ties—holding to nothing
They shun no wrong

507 It brings all folly—fond trust in any
Who lack knowledge

508 One who trusts others without trial—trouble
For generations on end

509 Trust no one untried—once tried entrust
With what one entrusts

510 Trust without trial—doubt of one tried—both
Yield trouble without end

52. KNOWING AND ENGAGING

511 One perceiving right and wrong whose nature
Seeks right—worthy to engage

512 One who fosters fecundity increases increase and studies
What hinders—engage

513 Clarity knowledge love the absence of greed—trust
Those filled with these four

514 Though tested in all ways many
Prove otherwise in action

515 Engage no one dear to one's heart unless they know
And endure action

516 Discern the doer discern the deed determine
The time and have done

517 This by this man and these means—in seeing it
Leave it to him

518 Having discerned who is fit for which deed let them
Make it their own

519 Fortune flees those taking amiss one freely
And fully in action

520 King—discern daily—when doers don't swerve
The world doesn't swerve

53. KINDNESS TO KINDRED

521 Even when one has nothing—kin celebrate
Ties over time

522 If one has kin of affection that endures one finds
Wealth that flourishes

523 Living without moving with family—like filling
A lake with no banks

524 Fruit that one gains in gaining wealth—family
Flowing freely on all sides

525 One who commands generosity and sweet words finds family
Upon family on all sides

526 The greatly generous who nurse no anger—
No better kin in the vast world

527 Crows conceal nothing and call and eat—those
Who are like them know wealth

528 That king who sees eminence not sameness—many
Thrive in his sight

529 When the cause for leaving has left—kinship
Returns of its own

530 A king should study reflect and welcome
Those who return for good cause

54. ABSENCE OF MIND

531 Worse even than unrestrained anger—neglect
From too much rejoicing

532 Absence of mind kills renown—as having
To fill daily kills knowledge

533 All the world's authors agree—no name
Without presence of mind

534 No stronghold for one who has fear—no refuge
With absence of mind

535 Those who fail to protect beforehand
Grieve the error after

536 If one never falls into failings with anyone
At any point—that is peerless

537 If one guards action with presence of mind there is nothing
That is not possible

538 What is honored do—even seven births
Cannot atone for not doing

539 If swelling with satisfaction remember
The forgetful who fell

540 One easily enacts one's thoughts
If one keeps thinking

55. GOOD RULE

541 Regal with all reflecting clear-eyed and doing
What is right—that is the way of justice

542 The world looks to the sky for life—as people
To the justice of a king

543 Virtue and the books of priests—both rest
On the rule of kings

544 The world embraces the feet of great kings whose rule
Embraces their people

545 Where kings rule as wisdom decrees
Rain and harvest abound

546 Not the king's spear but his rule grants victory—if
His rule does not bend

547 The king protects the world and justice protects the king—if
The king doesn't impede it

548 The king who sees no one and rectifies nothing
Sinks and ruins himself

549 Not a taint on a king but his task—correcting the people
He loves and protects

550 Like one weeding a crop as it grows—the king who punishes
Iniquity with death

56. HARSH RULE

551 Kings who torment accustomed to wrong—far
More cruel than killers

552 Like demanding with a spear—begging
With scepter in hand

553 The king who fails to do justice each day—each day
His country falls

554 He loses prosperity and people alike—the king
Without thought whose rule bends

555 The tears of the hopeless—force
That scrapes away riches

556 What lasts is good rule—without it
A king has no light

557 How is earth without rainfall—that's life
Without mercy in one's king

558 Beneath the rule of a king without justice
Having is worse than not having

559 When kings veer from justice—monsoons veer
From spilling their rains

560 Cows cease giving and the learned forget books
When guardians fail to guard

57. STRIKING NO FEAR

561 Discerning what is fitting and correcting
Completely—that is a king

562 For abundance to abound wield fiercely
And discharge gently

563 A tyrant feared for his deeds falls quickly
Without fail

564 If bitter words call him cruel a king crumbles
And falls quickly

565 A ghost seems to hold his riches—the mean-faced king
Whom no one can see

566 If one lacks eyes and speaks harshly—endless wealth
Ends in an instant

567 Harsh words and undue punishments—rasp
That erodes a king's mettle

568 If kings who spurn thought and counsel condemn
In anger—their fortunes decline

569 In battle he falls in the heat of terror—the king
Who creates no safety

570 Harsh rule that brings idiots together—nothing
Burdens the earth more

58. EYES THAT ARE MOVED

571 The astonishing beauty of eyes that are moved—because
It exists this world exists

572 The world has being because eyes are moved—without it
Men burden the earth

573 What good is a song that cannot be sung—what good is an eye
That cannot be moved

574 Beyond appearing in a face what good is an eye
If it cannot be moved in measure

575 Being moved adorns eyes—otherwise
They are nothing but sores

576 Like trees that are stuck in the ground—those stuck with eyes
That cannot be moved

577 Without eyes that are moved a person lacks eyes—with eyes
One never lacks movement

578 The virtuous king whose eyes can be moved—
This world belongs to him

579 Eyes moved to patience in those able to punish—
Nothing stands higher

580 Even seeing the poured poison they drink—those seeking
The kindness all seek

59. ESPIONAGE

581 Spies and books of conscience—know these
As a king's two eyes

582 Knowing all that goes on in all moments for all—that
Is the work of a king

583 The king without spies not seeing what's true—nothing
Keeps him supreme

584 Studying those acting and those near and those far—that
Is spying

585 Appearing beyond doubt fearing no eye
Spilling nothing—that is a spy

586 Able to cross as an ascetic learn and yield
To nothing—that is a spy

587 Hearing what's hidden and knowing
Past doubt—that is a spy

588 Take what a spy spies through the spying
Of another spy

589 Where three spies agree lies clarity—procure
They don't know who's who

590 Honor no spy in the open—honoring
Brings out what's hidden

60. HAVING ENERGY

591 One who has has energy—without it
What does one have

592 Having is having volition—the having
Of things never lasts

593 They never lament they've lost wealth—those
Who have energy at hand

594 To those with unwavering energy—wealth
Asks the way and arrives

595 To the depth of the water the root of the lotus—to the height
Of one's energy one's height

596 Let thought aspire to the heights—even
Unachieved it achieves

597 Even stung by arrows the elephant stands tall—even stung
By failure the sturdy do not slacken

598 One without energy never gains it—the glory
Of giving to the world

599 Even the elephant immense and sharp-tusked
Fears the tiger's attack

600 Strength within is strength overflowing—those
Without it are trees not men

61. FREEDOM FROM SLOTH

601 The undying light of one's family disappears
If sloth overtakes the flame

602 One who wants family to rise as family
Proceeds by slothing sloth

603 His family precedes him in falling—the fool
With sloth within

604 Their faults increase—their families fall—those fallen
To sloth failing to strive

605 Prolonging forgetting idling sleeping—vessel
Cherished by the falling

606 Even with land that lavishes wealth the idle
Attain nothing great

607 They'll hear scorn and thunder—those failing
To strive loving sloth

608 One soon turns slave to one's enemies if sloth
Inhabits one's family

609 If one evades sloth's rule the faults ruling
One's family are finished

610 The king free of sloth gains everything measured
By him who measured the worlds

62. MASTERY OF ACTION

611 Effort yields greatness—never droop thinking
Something is hard

612 Do not fail to do when doing—the world stays with those
Who stay to the end

613 Generosity's glory abides in the excellent
Command of energy

614 Generosity fails in men without energy like swords
In the hands of softlings

615 One who seeks action not pleasure—a pillar
Who frees family from suffering

616 Effort creates wealth—lack of effort
Installs lack

617 Misfortune lodges in sloth—fortune
Upon her flower in energy

618 Having no luck is no shame—having knowledge
Without action is shame

619 Even if fate adds nothing effort
Pays the body's labor

620 Those who strive without ceasing or despair
See the defeat of fate

63. NOT BEING DEFEATED BY ADVERSITY

621 Smile at adversity—nothing
Triumphs more fully

622 When the wise look within—the flood
Of adversity vanishes

623 Those untroubled by trouble give
Trouble to trouble

624 Besetting those like an ox on rough ground
Affliction gains affliction

625 Besetting those untroubled by its waves
Affliction afflicts affliction

626 Those who don't grasp and say it's all ours—do they suffer
And say we have nothing

627 The wise knowing woes will target the body
Take no distress as affliction

628 One suffers no suffering not longing for pleasure
And knowing that pain is natural

629 Not seeking pleasure in pleasure one finds
No suffering in suffering

630 Those who take pain as pleasure find prominence
Honored by enemies

II THE ARMS OF GOVERNMENT

64. MINISTERS

631 Great in means in method in timing and in action—
That is a minister

632 Greatness in these five—courage learning wisdom protection
Perseverance—that is a minister

633 Able to divide reunite cherish and keep—
That is a minister

634 Able to discern to act from discernment and to speak
Resolutely—that is a minister

635 One that knows right action sees what is possible and speaks
The fullest words—that is a worthy advisor

636 Before a learned and subtle mind
What subtlety can last

637 Even one who knows action must act knowing
The nature of the world

638 Though a king without knowledge kills knowledge those
Beside him must speak true

639 A million million enemies—better than a minister
Plotting wrong at one's side

640 Even planning perfectly ministers without mastery
Complete nothing

65. STRENGTH IN SPEECH

641 Excellence of the tongue is excellence—an excellence
Beyond all other excellence

642 They yield prosperity or ruin—watch
For weakness in one's words

643 To bind those listening and attract those
Not listening—that is speech

644 No victory or virtue is higher—know qualities
And speak

645 Speak knowing no speech can better
What you speak

646 Growing love by one's words—gaining good from others' words—principle
Of untarnished greatness

647 A mindful fearless master of words—hard
For anyone to overcome

648 When one attains sweetness and order in words—the world
Rushes to listen

649 Those who can't speak a few faultless words
Love to speak many words

650 Those who cannot convey learning—a cluster
Of flowers with no fragrance

66. PURITY OF ACTION

651 True allies impart wealth—true action—
All that one needs

652 Shun always all action that bears
No goodness or name

653 Steer clear of all deeds that dim light—you
Who would keep becoming

654 Those steady in vision do nothing disgraceful
Even in difficult times

655 Do nothing to regret—but if you do
Do not regret it

656 Though you watch your own mother starve
Do nothing the wise condemn

657 The greatest destitution of the wise—far above
All wealth gained by wrong

658 Those who spurn the spurning of deeds—even
Succeeding they suffer

659 What comes by tears goes by tears—even in loss
Goodness yields fruit in time

660 Like filling an unfired pot with water—protecting
With ill-gotten wealth

67. FIRMNESS OF ACTION

661 Firmness of action is firmness of mind—
All else is else

662 The way of the wise—desisting from trouble
And losing no heart in trouble

663 Mastery reveals what is finished—revealing
In the middle brings misery

664 Saying—easy for anyone—doing
As said—hard

665 Firmness of action in those of great vision reaches the king
And inspires the whole

666 When those planning are steadfast
Plans happen as planned

667 Scorn none by size—there are some like the pin
In a great cart's wheel

668 Enact without waiting or wavering
Each action seen clearly

669 Even in toil enact boldly all action
That ends in joy

670 Those who don't prize firmness of action even when firm
Will never be prized

68. WAYS OF ACTION

671 Resolve is the end of debate—bad
To let resolve languish

672 Delay what is meant for delay—delay nothing
Not meant for delay

673 When possible it is good to act—when not
Seek possibility and act

674 On reflection we see the remnants of actions and enemies
Scorch like remnants of fire

675 Bring these five out of darkness and act—
Tools time place means deed

676 Effort impediments greatness of what's gained—study
These first then act

677 Know the mind that knows it completely—that is how
To complete an action

678 Completing one action with another—like binding
A bull elephant with another

679 More pressing than favors to friends—drawing
The sideless to one's side

680 Those of small places aware of what shakes them
When gainful yield to the great

69. DIPLOMACY

681 Born to good lineage—full of love—possessing qualities
A king loves—that is a diplomat

682 These three an ambassador cannot do without—love
Knowledge strength in speaking true

683 Scholars among scholars—those whose words
Conquer among conquerors

684 Wisdom appearance profound learning—send into action
Those rich in these three

685 One of lucid speech who brings delight shuns dross
And yields good—that is a diplomat

686 Fearless learned able to convey perceiving
Each moment—that is a diplomat

687 Highest of all—those who consider place and time
And speak what is needed

688 A true envoy is true in these three—courage
Loyalty purity of heart

689 The fearless whose words never falter—they
Can carry the word of the king

690 Even facing death a diplomat remains fearless
Facing what's best for his king

70. MOVING WITH KINGS

691 With irascible kings move like one who warms
By a fire—neither close nor far

692 In not seeking what is sought by kings one gains
Enduring wealth from kings

693 Guard against misdeeds if one guards—suspected
It is hard to come clean

694 In the presence of royalty desist from whispers
And shared smiles

695 Ask nothing eavesdrop on nothing but listen
When what's hidden is shared

696 Take note wait and without displeasure say pleasingly
What wants to be said

697 Speak what is gainful never what is not
Even when asked

698 Never slight the king's youth or kin—move
With the light that's here

699 They do nothing disfavored thinking they're favored—those
Whose wisdom won't waver

700 Liberty that enacts unkindness thinking
Of old friendship brings ruin

71. READING FACES

701 A jewel on the earth of undying seas—he
Who sees and notes the unsaid

702 Those who discern the heart without doubt deem
Equal to the gods

703 Those who see behind faces—give anything
To make them your own

704 Though his body looks the same he is different—he
Who notes the unsaid

705 He who can't see behind faces—of his organs
What good are his eyes

706 A crystal reflects its neighbor—as a face
The fullness of one's heart

707 What is more wise than a face—it puts forth
Rage and wonder

708 If one should find those who can see within
It is enough to face them

709 If one finds those who know the eye's ways
Eyes speak friendship and hostility

710 Measure of those who claim wisdom—none other
To see than their eyes

72. KNOWING AN AUDIENCE

711 You who are lucid and know words—know and address
Your audience with care

712 Know the occasion and speak with clarity—you
Who are wise and know words

713 They know neither words nor strength—those speaking
Ignorant of audience

714 Be brilliant before brilliance—and as simple
As chalk before simplicity

715 Greatest of great qualities—restraint that won't speak
Too early among the wise

716 Like falling from grace—slipping before people
Of deep knowledge

717 Among those able to discern faultless words the learning
Of the learned brings light

718 Like watering a plot where plants thrive—speaking
Before those who sense deeply

719 You who speak well before the wise—do not lapse
Into speech before the little

720 Pouring forth before those who aren't peers—like spilling
Ambrosia in the yard

73. NOT FEARING AN AUDIENCE

721 They never falter before a great audience—the lucid
Who know ways and words

722 Learned among the learned—those who convey learning
To the learned

723 Many die bravely on the battlefield—few
Stand fearless before an audience

724 Convey one's learning to the learned and attain
What's greater from those greater

725 To answer an audience without fear—know and master
The art of argument

726 What good is a sword for cowards—and what good
A book for those fearful of wise listeners

727 Like a softling's bright sword on the battlefield—the learning
Of one fearing an audience

728 Although they have studied they are fruitless—those who do not
Speak well before the wise

729 Worse than those who haven't learned—those who have learned
But fear wise assemblies

730 Though here they are gone—those fearful of the hall
Unable to convey learning

74. COUNTRY

731 The union of unfailing yields untarnished wealth and people
Of wisdom—that is a country

732 Great flourishing without ruin with wealth worthy
Of desire—that is a country

733 Able to bear every burden as it comes giving all
The king's due—that is a country

734 Harmony completely free of great hunger deadly enemies
And endless disease—that is a country

735 Absence of factions king-vexing outlaws and crippling
Inner enemies—that is a country

736 Country unknown to ruin with bounty that never shrinks
Even in ruin—best of all countries

737 A country's limbs—flowing water fertile mountains ground water
Surface water and safety

738 Wealth safety harvest happiness freedom from disease—these
Are a country's beauty

739 Countries that thrive with toil are not countries—countries that thrive
Without toil—countries

740 Even if everything fits it's no use if a king
Does not fit his country

75. FORTRESSES

741 Even for the mighty a fortress is fortune—and fortune
For those fearing attack

742 Possessed of shining water land hills and forests
Of stunning shade—that is a fortress

743 Height width strength invincibility—these four together
Authorities call safety

744 Large in size with little to defend able to defeat
The ardor of enemies—that is a fortress

745 Hard to assail stocked up with food and easy
To hold within—that is a fortress

746 Provisioned with all things and warriors
At all points—that is safety

747 Hard to besiege storm or take by deceit—
That is a fortress

748 Where those who hold it hold off the highest
Of sieges—that is a fortress

749 Able to grant victory and glory at the outset
Of battle—that is a fortress

750 Even with every greatness without men of great action
A fortress is nothing

76. THE MAKING OF WEALTH

751 There is no other wealth than wealth to make
The worthless worthy

752 Those with nothing are scorned by all—those with wealth
Are honored

753 It conquers the darkness everywhere it goes—
The unfailing light of wealth

754 It grants both virtue and pleasure—wealth
Gained aright without harm

755 Shun absolutely the making of wealth that comes
Without mercy or love

756 The king's wealth—wealth levied wealth claimed
And wealth seized from enemies

757 Because wealth is its nurse mercy the babe
Born of love can thrive

758 Like watching elephants fighting from a hill—
Acting with wealth growing at hand

759 Make wealth—no blade severs more sharply
An enemy's pride

760 For one who is solid in wealth that shines
The other two come easy

77. THE SPLENDOR OF ARMIES

761 The king's highest holding—an army that conquers
Full of all force fearless of wounds

762 Except in an army of long lineage hard to find courage
That fears no danger or loss

763 So what if rats roar like the sea—with one hiss
Of a snake they're gone

764 Courage without defeat or corruption carried
Through time—that is an army

765 Force that gathers and fights though death rages
Upon it—that is an army

766 Courage nobility tradition assurance—these
Are an army's armor

767 Advancing fully in force withstanding
Advances—that is an army

768 Even unable to defeat or defend by its bearing
An army bears glory

769 Free of smallness lack and ceaseless aversion
An army prevails

770 Even with countless warriors—without captains
An army is nothing

78. THE VALOR OF WARRIORS

771 Scores that stood before him stand as stone—enemies
Stand not before my lord

772 Far sweeter bearing the spear that missed an elephant
Than the arrow that hit a forest hare

773 Valor it is said is ruthless—but nobility
Among the fallen is its edge

774 Routing an elephant with his spear he laughs
Pulling another from his body

775 If the fierce eyes of a warrior blink at a flying spear
His heart has already fled

776 In counting one's days every day without
Battle wounds means nothing

777 For those who seek fame not life the band
Of a warrior grants beauty

778 Warriors that do not fear death do not shrink
Even if a king rages

779 Heroes who die upholding their vows—who
Can call them little

780 Death is worth begging for if dying
Brings tears to a king's eyes

79. FRIENDSHIP

781 What is rarer than friendship—or greater
Protection against foes

782 Friendship with wise souls—a moon waxing—fellowship
With fools—a moon waning

783 Like relishing and relishing good books—relating
And relating to the wise

784 Not for laughter the making of friends but thunder
When going too far

785 Not presence not birth but feeling
Grants friendship its right

786 Friendship is not a face smiling—friendship
Is a heart that smiles

787 Friendship averts trouble shows the way and when
Trouble comes stays

788 Like hands that check a garment as it slips—friendship
Ends trouble in time

789 What is the throne of friendship—unwavering
Support in all ways

790 He is this to me—I am this to him—even
Saying this shrinks friendship

80. EXAMINED FRIENDSHIP

791 No greater ruin than thoughtless friendship—befriended
Friends cannot flee

792 Bonds made without thought upon thought
Bring mortal torment in the end

793 Consider character family errors and undying
Relations—then befriend

794 Those of good family who fear wrongdoing—befriend
Even by giving

795 Find and befriend them—those able to scorn wrong
Bring tears and set right

796 It measures one's friends—even torment
Contains merit

797 This is called profit to a man—avoiding
The friendship of fools

798 Befriend no one who flees in misfortune—take nothing
To heart that shrinks heart

799 The bond abandoned in adversity—even
At death it burns

800 Cherish friendship with the faultless and even with gifts
Renounce the unfit

81. LONG FRIENDSHIP

801 What is long friendship—friendship
That hinders no liberty

802 Liberties are the limbs of friendship—and to savor them
The duty of wisdom

803 If one cannot take the liberties friends take
What good is any long friendship

804 The liberties friends take without asking—the great
Take them with pleasure

805 Take it as folly or great liberty
If a friend offends

806 Even in injury friends in friendship reject no friendship
Faithful over time

807 Even when wronged those who love friends
Do not cease to love

808 It is a great day when a friend does wrong for those free
Not to hear a friend's wrongs

809 The wise love the friend who abandons no friendship
Enduring intact over time

810 Those true to friendship over time—even those
Who don't love them love them

82. HARMFUL FRIENDSHIP

811 With friends who lack goodness but seem essential it is better
Bonds shrink than grow

812 Friends who fit nothing friendly in fortune fleeting in famine—
so what
If one gains or loses them

813 Friendship that weighs gain—equal to thieves
And lovers for pay

814 Better to be alone than have friends who buckle
Like colts in battle

815 The paltry friend who offers no help—better
Not to have than to have

816 The ill will of the wise—a billion times better than
The grasping friendship of a fool

817 The gain of enmity—ten billion times greater than
The friendship of mere fun

818 With those insisting the possible is impossible
Let friendship slip silently away

819 Friends whose words and deeds never meet—bitter
Even in dreams

820 With those friendly at home but harsh in public—shun
The tiniest proximity

83. FALSE FRIENDSHIP

821 Friendship with false men—anvil
Waiting to be struck

822 Like women of two minds—bonds of kinship
Without kinship

823 Even studying many noble books the ignoble
Do not become noble

824 False men with sweet faces and hearts
That scowl—fear them

825 Those whose hearts do not meet ours—nothing
They say can be trusted

826 One knows quickly the words of foes though they speak
Good things like friends

827 The bow bowing betrays evil—heed not
An enemy's bowing words

828 The tears of foes—like hands in prayer
Hiding knives

829 Kill it within delighting without—friendship
With scorners who feign love

830 When foes act like friends be friendly
In face not heart

84. FOLLY

831 What to call folly—discarding what helps
And keeping what hurts

832 Folly of follies—to love deeds unfit
For one's hands

833 Absence of shame affection attention or care for anything—
That is the work of folly

834 No greater fool than he who studies knows and advises
Without governing himself

835 The hell for seven lives of wrong—a fool
Attains it in one

836 Failure and fetters when a fool without skill
Attempts action

837 Strangers feast and relations starve if a fool
Should chance on fortune

838 Like madmen getting drunk—a fool getting
Anything in his hands

839 At parting no pain—how lovely
The friendship of fools

840 The fool entering wise company—like going to bed
With one's backside unwashed

85. PRESUMPTION

841 Want in want is want of knowledge—for wisdom
No other want is want

842 If fools give happily it is the tavam
Of those receiving

843 Afflictions afflicted by fools on themselves—hard even
For enemies to equal

844 What to call ignorance—the arrogance
That says we know

845 Learning without faults falls into doubt pretending
To learning unlearned

846 With all faults exposed presumption
Puts on a fig leaf

847 They bring themselves woe—the ignorant
Ignoring wise counsel

848 Those who heed none nor see for themselves—
Till death their life is a plague

849 One teaching the sightless is sightless—the sightless
See as they've seen

850 Those who deny what the wise say—specters
Haunting the earth

86. DISCORD

851 Discord—disease that breeds unnatural division
Among all lives

852 Highest not to return evil in discord even if
Aggrieved by division

853 It yields unfettered and unending light—ending
The disease of discord

854 The joy of joys blossoms when discord
Woe of woes disappears

855 Who can defeat them—those whose forbearance
Defeats discord

856 The life that delights in division—poised
On poverty and oblivion

857 The bitter who bring discord do not see
The truth that brings triumph

858 To desist from discord brings wealth—to abet it
Abets destruction

859 In abundance one sees no discord—in ruin
One sees its rise

860 Discord occasions all bitterness—concord
The peak of goodness

87. SPLENDOR FOR ENEMIES

861 Nurture no strife with those stronger—welcome
Contention with those weaker

862 Without love without strength without strong friends
How can one defeat enemies

863 Those fearful witless friendless ungiving—
Easy prey for enemies

864 Easy for anyone anytime anywhere—the constantly angry
Who cannot keep secrets

865 A delight to enemies—those with no goodness who seek no way
See no shame and miss all chances

866 They will find their hostility hosted—those
With blind rage and inordinate desire

867 Those who obstruct what they start—attain their enmity
Even with gifts

868 They strengthen their enemies and lack friends—those
With much vice and no virtue

869 For those with fearful and ignorant foes
Joy is never out of reach

870 No fame attends failing to contend against little
And angry fools

88. KNOWING AN ENEMY

871 The kindlessness of enmity—not fit to wish for
Even in jest

872 Oppose those who plow with bows—not those
Who plow with words

873 Madder than madness is to make
Many enemies alone

874 Those whose kindness turns enmity to friendship—the world
Lives by their light

875 When alone with two enemies choose one
To be a dear friend

876 Whether trusted or not neither trust
Nor forsake one in trouble

877 Show no weakness to enemies—nor woes
To friends who can't see them

878 Perceive strengthen and guard oneself and the pride
Of one's enemies dies

879 Cut down brambles when small—grown
They cut the cutting hand

880 One breath and they're gone—those who haven't toppled
A foe's pride

89. ENEMIES WITHIN

881 Water and shade become bitter when bitter—relations
Grow bitter by bitter deeds

882 Fear no enemies who appear like swords—fear enemies
Who appear like kin

883 Guard against enemies within—unguarded they cleave
Like knives through clay

884 If false-hearted enemies appear within they bring
Great misery among kin

885 If enemies appear among kin they bring
Many miseries that kill

886 If oneness disappears among one's own
Hard ever to escape death

887 Even appearing like pot and lid enemies
In family fit nothing

888 Like a rasp upon metal enemies within family
Wear all of it away

889 Even if only the splinter of a seed enmity
Within breeds ruin

890 Like living in a hut with snakes—life
With those without concord

90. NOT SCORNING THE GREAT

891 Greatest protection for those that protect—not slighting
The might of the mighty

892 One gains great suffering from the great
In failing to respect the great

893 If one seeks ruin act without listening—if one seeks death
Offend those above

894 Like summoning death—offending the mighty
Without having might

895 Those who anger a king of cruel power—anywhere
They go they're gone

896 Those who get burned can recover—those
Who scorn the great cannot

897 What good are royal trappings and infinite wealth
If the great in virtue grow angry

898 If those like mountains think it—those seeming to tower
Disappear with their kin

899 If the highest in virtue are angered—even
The king of the gods falls

900 Even with allies beyond measure one cannot escape
If the greatest of the great grow angry

91. YIELDING TO WIVES

901 No virtue in craving one's wife—it is something unsought
By those who crave deeds

902 The wealth of one craving his wife without care
Brings shame on himself and all men

903 Among good people it always brings shame—losing
Oneself to one's wife

904 One gaining no glory fearing his wife
Gains no mastery of deeds

905 One fearing his wife fears to do good
To good people at all times

906 One fearing the bamboo shoulders of his wife
Even living like a god has nothing

907 Modesty in a woman is far more glorious
Than servility in a man

908 They do no good nor help their friends—those
Who follow their wives' brows

909 For him who does only his wife's bidding—no virtue
No wealth no pleasure

910 A mind in place at work never knows the folly
Of following one's wife

92. LIMITLESS WOMEN

911 They lead to ruin—the sweet words of well-bangled women
Who seek money not love

912 Weigh good and stay clear of heartless women
Speaking of heart but weighing gain

913 The false embrace of one selling herself—like gripping
Some corpse in the dark

914 The wise seeking grace do not seek the thin pleasure
Of those who seek only things

915 The wise of good minds do not seek the thin pleasure
Of those whose goods are common

916 Those extending their goodness do not seek skilled arms
Extending thin pleasures

917 Those without full hearts seek arms that embrace
With hearts elsewhere

918 The embrace of false women—siren to those
Without sense

919 The arms of women with jewels and no limits—hell
Where heedless men sink

920 Consorts to those abandoned by fortune—dice
Drink women of two minds

93. NOT DRINKING

921 They inspire no fear—they lose their glory—men
Drowning in drink

922 Drink no drink but know if you do the wise
Will see you as nothing

923 Ugly even before one's mother—what then
Being drunk before the wise

924 On those who commit the vile error of drinking
Modesty turns her back

925 Paying to be out of one's head—that is born
Of not knowing one's way

926 The sleeping and the dead are not different—nor those
Drinking poison and those drunk

927 Those drinking in secret eyes drooping—laughed at always
By neighbors who see

928 No use saying I have never drunk—with drink
What's hidden comes out

929 Arguing with a drunkard—like searching for a man
Beneath water with a candle

930 When a man isn't drunk does he not see drink's stupor
Seeing another man drink

94. DICE

931 Desire no dice though you might win—winning
Is the hook the fish swallows

932 Do players who win one and lose one hundred have a way
To thrive and win goodness

933 Their wealth and revenue roll away—those
Who roll dice without ceasing

934 Dicing ruins reputations and brings many miseries—
Nothing impoverishes faster

935 The greedy seeking dice dice halls and dice hands
Devolve into nothing

936 Their bellies never fill—torments torment them—those swallowed
By the woe of dice

937 Consigning one's time to the table old wealth
And character disappear

938 Dicing destroys wealth afflicts anguish destroys goodness
And makes a person a lie

939 If one takes to tables—no wealth no food no clothing
No learning no light

940 As a player clings to dice in losing—life
Clings to body in suffering

95. MEDICINE

941 Disease comes of too little or too much through the trio
With wind named by authors

942 The body needs no medicine if one eats
Only after digestion

943 Eat after digestion knowing one's limits—this way
Those with a body live long

944 After digesting wait for hunger then savor with care
What does not disagree

945 If one eats with measure what does not disagree
Nothing threatens one's life

946 Those who eat knowing moderation know joy—as those
Who devour know disease

947 Those who devour beyond their fire's limit
Know disease beyond limit

948 Determine disease determine its cause determine its cure
And cure unerringly

949 Time patient and disease—doctors perceive these
In measure and proceed

950 Healer patient medicine preparer—these four
Together are medicine

III ALL ELSE

96. LINEAGE

951 Natural only to those born to a home—modesty
And morality together

952 Modesty conduct truthfulness—those born to a family
Never slip from these three

953 Generosity cheer sweet words lack of scorn—these four
Arise from true family

954 Even with millions upon millions those born to a family
Do nothing demeaning

955 Even if their means of giving have fallen a long-standing family
Does not fall from its nature

956 Those who uphold a faultless family do nothing
Unfitting or false

957 Like a stain on the bright moon above—a flaw
In one born to a family

958 If he has no kindness among his virtues the birth
Of a man falls into doubt

959 As seedlings reveal the soil—words spoken
Reveal one's family

960 If one seeks goodness seek modesty—if one seeks family
Seek humility with all

97. HONOR

961 However indispensable renounce anything
That diminishes

962 Even for glory those who seek glorious command
Do nothing inglorious

963 In adversity stand tall—in prosperity
Remain humble

964 Like hair fallen from one's head—a man
Fallen from his place

965 In descending to even the most minuscule diminishment
Mountains diminish

966 It leads to neither name nor heaven—
Why flatter those who scorn

967 Better to be dead and standing than trailing
Detractors and living

968 If one's greatness of honor is gone is guarding
One's body a remedy

969 They give up life for honor—those like the deer that dies
If one hair gets lost

970 Those who won't live without honor—the world
Worships their light

98. GREATNESS

971 Aspiration is glory—saying we can live
Without it—disgrace

972 Birth is common to all—greatness born
Of great deeds is not

973 Those without highness even high are not high—those without lowness
Even low are not low

974 Like women of one mind a person is great
Only by ruling oneself

975 The great enact the impossible
Rightly and fully

976 The small do not know it—the desire to honor
And emulate the great

977 When acclaim befalls those without eminence
It leads to insolent action

978 Smallness adores and adorns itself—greatness
Is always humble

979 Greatness is absence of arrogance—smallness
Is arrogance everywhere

980 Greatness shields failings—smallness
Proclaims every fault

99. INTEGRITY

981 For those upholding integrity knowing what fits
Everything good is natural

982 Goodness for the wise—goodness of character—good
Beyond all other goods

983 Modesty truth compassion love kindness—these five
Are the bedrock of integrity

984 Tavam is not killing—and integrity
Is not speaking ill of others

985 The strength of the strong is humility—with it
The wise transform foes

986 Touchstone of integrity—accepting defeat
Even against unequals

987 If one does nothing good to those not doing good
What good is integrity

988 If one attains the strength of integrity
Poverty is no disgrace

989 Those called oceans of integrity never crumble
Though time itself crumbles

990 If those with integrity lose their integrity the wide earth
Cannot bear the burden

100. HAVING KINDNESS

991 From openness to all people the practice
Of kindness comes easily

992 Love in one's heart and birth in good family together
Are the way of kindness

993 Likeness in limbs is not likeness in people—likeness is likeness
In kindness overflowing

994 Those who serve with justice and goodness—the world
Celebrates their kind

995 Even in jest scorn is bitter—even in strife
The kind remain kind

996 The world exists because people have kindness—if not
It would plummet into dust

997 Even as sharp as a blade—without human kindness
Men are blocks of wood

998 Even toward the unfriendly who do wrong it is last
To be unkindly

999 For those who cannot smile—even in daylight the great
Wide world is darkness

1000 Riches attained by those without kindness—like milk
Soured by its jug

101. FRUITLESS WEALTH

1001 Dead with nothing left to do—those who've gathered
Great wealth without tasting it

1002 The confusion of grasping saying wealth yields all
Yields an ugly birth

1003 Their birth burdens the earth—men hungry to earn
Who seek no renown

1004 One no one loves—what does he think
He will leave behind

1005 Those who won't give and enjoy—even with billions
They have nothing

1006 If one won't enjoy it nor give to the worthy
The greatest wealth is misery

1007 Wealth ungiven to those without—like a woman of great goodness
Growing old alone

1008 The wealth of one unloved—a poisonous tree
Bearing fruit in the square

1009 Others will take it—all wealth amassed
Without love enjoyment and virtue

1010 A moment of want for the worthy with wealth—merely rain
Dried up for a time

102. HAVING MODESTY

1011 Modesty in action is modesty—different from the modesty
Of fine women whose brows shine

1012 All may have food and clothing and such—the great
Alone have modesty

1013 All lives entail bodies—all integrity
The goodness of modesty

1014 Is not modesty a jewel for the wise—and without it
Is not pride an affliction

1015 Those who fear shame in themselves and others—there
Dwells modesty say the wise

1016 Without the shield of modesty the great do not want even
The wide world

1017 Those who command modesty renounce life
For modesty—not modesty for life

1018 If a man feels no shame for what shames others
Virtue itself feels shame

1019 Errors in conduct sear family—absence of shame
Sears all that is good

1020 Those moving without modesty—like puppets
Alive only with strings

103. SERVING FAMILY

1021 No greater glory than greatness in action saying
I won't ever cease

1022 Mastery of action fullness of knowledge—these
Two thriving make family thrive

1023 For one saying I will raise up my family—divinity
Girds up its loins and sets forth

1024 For those who strive for family without ceasing—success
Obtains without planning

1025 Those without fault whose lives serve family—the wise
Encircle them as kin

1026 To command the family of one's birth—that
Is worthy command

1027 Like the strong-hearted in battle—those able in family
Bear the weight

1028 There is no season for serving one's family—
Dally in pride and it's gone

1029 The bodies of those who keep family from fault—are they only
Vessels for suffering

1030 Without a good person to keep family upright
Adversity fells it at its root

104. FARMING

1031 Turn as it will the world follows the plow—toil as one might
Farming is highest

1032 Farmers sustain everyone not farming—they
Are the pin holding the world together

1033 They live who live by farming—all others
Follow and honor them for food

1034 They see many shelters beneath their king's shelter—
Those whose fields shelter grain

1035 He who eats by his own hand does not beg
And gives freely to beggars

1036 If farmers fold their arms those saying
I need nothing cannot be

1037 If one dries it to one-fourth soil flourishes without even
One handful of manure

1038 Better than plowing is spreading manure—better than water is watching
The crops once weeded

1039 If its husbandman stays away the land pulls back
And sulks like a wife

1040 The good earth laughs if she sees idle men
Saying they have nothing

105. WANT

1041 What is as bitter as want—want alone
Is as bitter as want

1042 Want is a wretch—it leaves one in want
Here and hereafter

1043 The craving of want ruins long lineage
And loveliness alike

1044 Even in those born to a family want yields despair
That breeds vile words

1045 Of the suffering that is want
Misery on misery arises

1046 Even if the destitute know and speak truth
Their words falter and fail

1047 Want without virtue makes one a stranger even
To one's own mother

1048 The lack that almost killed yesterday—
Will it get me today

1049 One may sleep among flames but in poverty
One's eyes find no rest

1050 Death to gruel and salt—those with nothing
Who will not let go

106. BEGGING

1051 Seeing those fit for begging beg—refusing
Is their fault not yours

1052 If what one begs brings no misery—begging
Too is pleasure

1053 Before those who know duty whose hearts withhold nothing
Begging has beauty

1054 From those who deny nothing even in dreams begging
Is equal to giving

1055 Because some on earth deny nothing—one
May stand in sight begging

1056 Seeing those with no woe of withholding
All woes of poverty disappear

1057 Seeing people who give without scorn
The heart rejoices within

1058 If there were no beggars in this great and green world
Only puppets would come and go

1059 What splendor would the generous possess
If no one undertook to beg

1060 A beggar should bear no anger—the woe of poverty
Bears witness enough

107. DREAD OF BEGGING

1061 Even before eyes that delight in giving—ten million times better
Not to beg

1062 If people must beg to live—may the maker
Of this world perish

1063 No harshness more harsh than saying we'll end
This hardship by begging

1064 The greatness of those with nothing who won't beg—
Nothing can contain it

1065 Nothing sweeter than eating by one's labor—even
If nothing but broth

1066 Nothing scorns a tongue more than begging—even
To beg water for a cow

1067 I beg all who beg—beg if you must but never
From those who won't give

1068 It shatters on the rock of refusal—the unsheltered
Raft of begging

1069 Hearts wilt at the thought of begging—and die utterly
At the thought of refusal

1070 Where can those who refuse hide—with a word
A beggar's life passes

108. WICKEDNESS

1071 The wicked appear so human—no others
Look more like men

1072 The wicked are luckier than the good—nothing
Troubles their hearts

1073 The wicked are like gods—they too
Do as they please

1074 When the vicious see villains they delight
In outdoing them

1075 Fear is the code of villains—and avarice
A little if there

1076 The wicked are like drums—they broadcast
Every secret they hear

1077 The wet hands of the wicked do not open except
To fists that crack jaws

1078 The wise respond to one word—the vicious
To being crushed like cane

1079 Seeing the food and clothing of others the wicked
Seek out their faults

1080 What else are the wicked for—in hardship they rush
To sell themselves

PART THREE

LOVE

I SECRET LOVE

109. ALLURE

1081 Is she a siren a rare peacock a woman in jewels—
My heart quakes

1082 As if on attack with an army of sirens—the look
She gives when I look

1083 I did not know death but now I do—
Fierce feminine eyes

1084 They don't fit this young woman—these eyes
That kill those looking

1085 Is it death an eye a deer—her gaze
Contains all three

1086 If they did not curve from her eyes her brows
Would not make me tremble

1087 The clothing covering her breasts—like blinders that keep
An elephant calm

1088 Feared in battle by foes my strength has fallen
To this forehead of light

1089 Why all these jewels on this doe-eyed girl
Already adorned in modesty

1090 Drink delights those drinking—not love
Which delights those looking

110. KNOWING SIGNS

1091 Two looks in her eyelined eyes—one that brings illness
And one that heals it

1092 Furtive and fleeting glances—not half of love—
Far more

1093 She looked and looked down—that is how
She watered affection

1094 When I look she looks at the ground—when I don't
She looks smiling softly

1095 Without seeming to look she smiles as if
Winking an eye

1096 Though they speak like strangers one sees
When words lack malice

1097 Words that seem harsh—looks that seem cross—sign
That those apart are together

1098 Her slenderness hints at hope—I look and her kindness
Graces with a smile

1099 Looks as among strangers—found only
Among lovers

1100 When eyes meet eyes mouths that speak
Mean nothing

111. THE JOYS OF JOINING

1101 Sight sound taste touch smell—in this shining jewel
I know all five

1102 Ailment is other than cure—but this beauty
Cures the ailment she causes

1103 Can the world of the lotus-eyed god be sweeter
Than sleep in my love's soft arms

1104 It cools when near and burns when far—where
Did she get this fire

1105 Like all one desires at once—her arms
And her braid of flowers

1106 They are made of ambrosia—each time her arms touch me
I come alive

1107 The embrace of this golden girl—like feasting with guests
In one's home

1108 Sweetest for lovers—an embrace without
Room for air

1109 Turning returning reuniting—these are the fruits
Of those joined in love

1110 Like the unknowing we know the more that we know—my love
For this jewel the more that we join

112. IN PRAISE OF HER

1111 Live long most delicate anicham—she whom I love
Is more delicate than you

1112 You swoon at flowers my heart—thinking flowers
That anyone sees are her eyes

1113 Her smile—pearls—her arms—bamboo—her smell—perfume—
Her body—new leaves—and her dark eyes—lances

1114 If water lilies could see they would look to the ground
Unable to match this beauty's eyes

1115 No good drums for her waist—she wore
An anicham with its stem

1116 The stars wander from their places not knowing
The moon from her face

1117 Does her face have flaws like the pockmarked moon
Shining only when full

1118 Moon live long—if you shone like her face you too
Would have my love

1119 Moon—to equal her face with her eyes like flowers
Do not appear to so many

1120 Anicham petals and swan feathers—berries of thorns
To her feet

113. IN PRAISE OF LOVE

1121 She of soft words—what glistens on her teeth
Is milk mixed with honey

1122 What connects body and breath—that
Connects me to her

1123 Image be gone from my eye—there isn't
Any room for the brow I love

1124 This jewel adorned in perfection—her presence is life
And her absence death

1125 I could remember her nature and bright warring eyes
If I forgot—but I can't forget

1126 Even if I blink he stays in my eyes unharmed—my love
So subtle and fine

1127 He dwells in my eyes so I do not paint them—I would not
Want to hide him

1128 He dwells in my heart so I fear hot food—I would not
Want him to get burned

1129 If I close my eyes he'll vanish—that's why this place
Calls him heartless

1130 He dwells forever with joy in my heart—but this place
Thinks he's heartless and gone

114. DOWN WITH DECORUM

1131 No way but this for those suffering love—the power
Of a horse made of palms

1132 Down with decorum—my body and soul cannot bear it
And will ride the palm

1133 Then I had power and proportion—now
I have the palmhorse of lovers

1134 The storm of love carries it away—the raft
Of proportion and power

1135 Gift from her with bangles like garlands—this misery
At twilight and this palm

1136 This girl keeps my eyes open—even at midnight
I think to ride the palm

1137 Nothing is greater than a woman—even suffering a sea of love
She mounts no palm

1138 Without pity or thought love entered the square
With our secret

1139 Love thought that none knew but now turns
Bewildered in the streets

1140 They laugh in my sight—the clueless
Who haven't felt what I feel

115. TALK

1141 People talk and dear life continues—by grace
Many don't know this

1142 Not knowing this girl of flower eyes is so rare the place talks
And gives her to me

1143 Even without having it I have it—isn't that
Because people talk

1144 This love grows on gossip—without it
It would shrivel and die

1145 Like desire for drink in drinking—the more people say
The sweeter the love

1146 We saw each other once but they talk like
A snake swallowed the moon

1147 With talk as manure and mother's words as water
This illness grows and grows

1148 Like dousing a fire with oil—dousing
This love with talk

1149 He that said not to worry left and shamed me—why
Be ashamed of rumor

1150 This place has talked as we'd wished—now
He'll wish to do right

II WEDDED LOVE

116. UNBEARABLE ABSENCE

1151 If not going tell me—if coming back quickly
Tell those still living

1152 His sight brought pleasure but fearing he'll go
His touch brings pain

1153 His words mean nothing—he knows
But parting still looms

1154 If he says not to worry and leaves—is it the fault
Of those who believed

1155 Avert his departure if one would avert—departed
There will be no reunion

1156 If his heart can tell me he's going—how
Can I hope he'll return

1157 Do these bangles that slip from my wrists not say
This captain is sailing

1158 It's bitter to live without sisters—and worse
Without him who was sweet

1159 Does fire which burns when touched burn
Like love abandoned

1160 Those who bear the unbearable—their hearts healed
The absence borne—there are so many

117. PINING AWAY

1161 I hide my ailment but it wells like water
To those drawing

1162 I cannot hide this ailment nor tell it without shame
To him ailing me

1163 Love and shame hang from the ends of my life
On a body that cannot bear it

1164 Right here the sea of love and no vessel
To cross it safely

1165 What would they bring in hatred—those
Bringing woe in love

1166 Love is an ocean of bliss but the pain
It brings is greater

1167 In love's vast waters I see no shore—no one but me
In the night

1168 With me alone for company it puts all other lives
To sleep—the night is so kind

1169 More cruel than his cruelties—these nights
That pass so slowly

1170 Could they go to him like my thoughts my eyes
Would not swim in tears

118. THE LONGINGS OF EYES

1171 They showed me the sight that ails me—why
Do these eyes weep

1172 These eyelined eyes that saw without seeing—why
Do they suffer without seeing

1173 These eyes that rushed to see now weep—
How laughable

1174 They've dried up from weeping—these eyelined eyes that brought
This endless disease

1175 These eyes that brought illness beyond oceans
Now suffer beyond sleep

1176 The eyes that brought me this illness
Now suffer it—how sweet

1177 May these eyes that loved and longed to see him
Weep and weep and dry up

1178 My loveless beloved is alive—but my eyes
Cannot rest without seeing him

1179 He goes they don't sleep he comes they don't sleep—torture
For eyes either way

1180 It's not hard for neighbors to know what's hidden
When you have drums for eyes like me

119. PALLOR

1181 I let my love leave—whom can I tell
How I've paled

1182 Because he gave love—this pallor
Spreads over my body

1183 He took beauty and modesty and gave
In return this sickness and pallor

1184 I think and speak his virtues alone and still
This pallor weasels in

1185 Look there—he goes—look here—this pallor
Comes to my body

1186 As darkness awaits the lamp going out this pallor awaits
His arms letting go

1187 I embraced I shifted and in only that shifting
This pallor took hold

1188 Everybody says she's pallid—nobody says
He left her

1189 May my body pale completely if my love
Remains well

1190 Good to bear the name pallid if no one
Calls my love loveless

120. THE ANGUISH OF SOLITUDE

1191 Those having the love of their beloved
Have love's fruit without stones

1192 Like rain to the living the gift a beloved
Gives his love

1193 Known only to lovers who are loved—the glory
Of saying we live

1194 If their beloved does not love them even
Those loved are loveless

1195 If he does not love—what does the one
We love give us

1196 Love with one side is bitter—with two balanced
Like a pole it is sweet

1197 Standing on one person's side does love not see
This torture and torment

1198 No hearts are harder than those living on earth
Without their beloved's sweet words

1199 Even if my beloved is loveless every word of him
Is sweet to my ear

1200 You tell your pain to him who won't hear—
Dear heart—close up the sea

121. THE LONGING OF MEMORY

1201 The thought alone brings endless delight—love
Is sweeter than wine

1202 All of love is sweet—remember your beloved
And nothing else matters

1203 Did he only seem to remember—this sneeze
Died before it came

1204 Am I there too in his heart—he
Is always in mine

1205 He locks me from his heart—does he feel
No shame to enter mine

1206 I live reliving our days—without that
How would I live

1207 I know no forgetting and each thought burns—what
Would happen if I forgot

1208 No matter my thought he never gets angry—how great
My lover's regard

1209 My sweet life withers thinking of his cruelty—he
Who said we weren't two

1210 Stay and shine dear moon—I would see him who left
Without leaving

122. TALK OF DREAMS

1211 This dream with its message from him—what
Can I offer it

1212 If my dark carp-like eyes would sleep when I begged
I could tell my love I endure

1213 My love with no love in life—I see him
In dreams and live

1214 Dreams give me love—they bring me
Him with no love in life

1215 Seeing him in dreams—as sweet in that moment
As seeing him in life

1216 If there wasn't this waking—the love in my dreams
Would never leave

1217 Why does this brute without love in life
Torment me so in dreams

1218 I sleep—he lies in my arms—I wake—
He's back in my heart

1219 They call him loveless in life—those
Who don't see him in dreams

1220 These people who say he's left me in life—
Do they not see him in dreams

123. THE MISERY OF EVENING

1221 You are not evening but the lance that ends wives—
Time—live long

1222 Is your husband hard-hearted like mine—bless you
You wretched bewildering evening

1223 This evening once pale and trembling now blossoms
As hardship and pain

1224 Without my beloved the evening arrives like a foe
On the field of death

1225 What evil did I do the evening—what good
Did I do the dawn

1226 Those moments with him I did not know
The miseries of evening

1227 At dawn it buds—all day it swells—and at dusk
It blossoms—this disease

1228 Battle-axe and emissary of evening ablaze—
The cowherd's flute

1229 When the evening baffles the senses sorrow
Will baffle this place

1230 As evening bewilders thinking of him who thinks only
Of wealth this endless life ends

124. THE DROOPING OF LIMBS

1231 Your eyes shy even from flowers thinking of him
Far off who left us in sadness

1232 They say our beloved does not love us—these eyes
Grown pale with tears

1233 They announce his absence—these shoulders
That swelled for your wedding

1234 When he left these arms lost their luster—now
They are losing their bangles

1235 These arms without luster or bangles
Proclaim this brute's brutality

1236 My arms and bangles slip but what hurts
Is calling him brutal

1237 By telling this brute the uproar of my arms
Would you gain honor my heart

1238 The brow of my love in bangles went pale
Even loosening my arms

1239 One puff of air entered our embrace and her eyes
Fresh as rain grew pale

1240 Seeing what her bright forehead could do the pallor
Of her eyes felt pain

125. TO HER HEART

1241 Heart—for this disease without end
Can you find no cure

1242 How stupid to suffer when he has
No love—bless you my heart

1243 He that brought this woe does not feel pity—
Why sit here and pine my heart

1244 They'll devour me longing to see him—take
My eyes with you my heart

1245 This love who does not love us—can we hate him
And leave him my heart

1246 You see him who soothes but fail to sulk—
Your anger is fake my heart

1247 Drop love or drop modesty good heart—
I cannot bear both

1248 How stupid my heart—you go to him thinking
He's loveless in ignorance

1249 Our love dwells within you—whom
Do you seek my heart

1250 If he who left me stays in my heart I'll lose
What beauty remains

126. LOSS OF RESTRAINT

1251 The door of restraint bolted with modesty—battered
By the axe of aching

1252 Love has no pity—even at midnight
My heart labors

1253 I hide my love but it comes out
Despite me like a sneeze

1254 I thought I had restraint but this love
Escapes into the open

1255 The dignity that won't follow them who've left—unknown
To those sick with love

1256 What a fine affliction—it wants me
To follow him who left

1257 I know nothing of shame when he does
What I love for love

1258 The forces that ruin my modesty—are they not
The sweet nothings of a fraud

1259 I went to sulk but instead embraced—my heart
Saw us conjoining

1260 We whose hearts melt like butter in fire—do we ever
Turn from his touch

127. LONGING TO REUNITE

1261 My eyes grow weak and lose luster—my fingers grow worn
Numbering the days he's been gone

1262 Glittering friend—if I forget him bangles and beauty
Will slip from my arms forever

1263 With his heart he left seeking gain—seeking
His return I'm still here

1264 My heart climbs higher and higher believing
He will come back with love

1265 May these eyes feast upon him—these lean shoulders
Will then cease to be pale

1266 I'll relish my love till all illness is gone—let him
Return for one day

1267 When my love dear as eyes returns will I sulk
Or welcome or take him

1268 May the king fight and win—that evening
I shall dine with my wife

1269 Each day is seven for those who await
A traveler's return

1270 What good to have or have had or hold
If one's heart is broken

128. MAKING SIGNS KNOWN

1271 Your dark eyes cannot hide it—they
Have something to say

1272 My bamboo-armed beauty who fills my eyes
Is being too much a lady

1273 Like thread between beads something
Shows in her beauty

1274 Like the fragrance in a budding blossom there is something
In her budding smile

1275 The secret singing of her bangles
Bears the remedy for my ills

1276 The passion and fire of his embrace
Tell me they'll disappear

1277 The coolness of my lover from cool shores—my bangles
Know it before I do

1278 My love left yesterday but my body
Has been pale for seven

1279 She looked at her bangles her arms her feet—
That's what she did

1280 Women among women—those whose eyes tell
The love that ails them

129. LONGING FOR UNION

1281 Rejoicing on thinking—delighting on looking—it happens
With love not wine

1282 When love surpasses the size of a tree no need
For one seed of sulking

1283 Though he does as he cares without care my eyes cannot rest
Without seeing my husband

1284 Friend—I went to sulk—but my heart went
To his side forgetting

1285 Like eyes that don't see the brush that paints them
I see no faults when I see him

1286 When seeing I see no failings—not seeing
I see nothing else

1287 Like one who jumps knowing the current—why sulk
Knowing its failure

1288 Great cheat—your chest is like wine—one drinks
Despite your disgrace

1289 Love is more fragile than a flower—few
Can meet its moment

1290 Her eyes withdrew but her arms embraced even
More eagerly than mine

130. AT ODDS WITH ONE'S HEART

1291 Heart—seeing that his heart is his
Why aren't you mine

1292 My heart—you see he's loveless yet go to him
Thinking he won't anger

1293 My heart—do you follow him to show
The ruined have no friends

1294 Heart—you savor without sulking—who
Will listen to you now

1295 My heart is endless heartache—it fears not having—
And having—fears losing

1296 When I am alone thinking my heart's here
To eat at me

1297 I forget all modesty with this feeble foolish heart
That will not forget him

1298 Ashamed to disdain him this heart clings to life
Dwelling on his goodness

1299 If one's own heart isn't a friend—who
Will befriend one in sorrow

1300 If one's own heart isn't kin it is nothing
That strangers aren't kind

131. SULKING

1301 Sulk and keep from his arms—let us
See him suffer a little

1302 Sulking is like salt—a little much
Is too much

1303 Fleeing without embracing the one sulking—like afflicting
The one afflicted

1304 Like severing the root of a withered vine—not turning
To those turned away

1305 Sulking in those with flower-like eyes
Is beauty even for the good

1306 Without quarrels or sulking love
Is a rotten or unripened fruit

1307 The sorrow of sulking—not knowing how long
The reunion will last

1308 Without a lover who sees that one suffers
What good is suffering

1309 Sulking in love is sweet—as water
In shade is sweet

1310 With one able to keep wasting away
My heart yearns only for union

132. SULKING'S SUBTLETIES

1311 The eyes of women feast on your chest—I will not
Lie with what's left

1312 I sulked and he sneezed thinking
I might say bless you

1313 If I wear a garland of new flowers she fumes
Saying I wear them for another

1314 I said that our love is greater than any and she sulked
Which any which any

1315 I said we won't part in this life—and her eyes
Overflowed with tears

1316 I remembered you I said and she pulled back—
So you forgot

1317 I sneezed and she blessed me—then wept
Saying who made you sneeze

1318 I held back a sneeze and she wept saying
Whose thought do you hide

1319 If I calm her she fumes saying you are like this
With them too aren't you

1320 If I gaze at her and think—she fumes saying
Who do you think of gazing

133. SULKING AND BLISS

1321 Though he's done no wrong pulling back
Brings him closer

1322 Though care at first may sag—sulking's small angers
Strengthen affection

1323 Hearts joined like earth and water—what heaven
Transcends their sulking

1324 Found in pulling from embraces—the forces
That open my heart

1325 Even free of wrong there is something in keeping
From my love's soft arms

1326 Sweeter than eating—having eaten—sweeter than loving—
Sulking in love

1327 When hearts come together we see it—in sulking
Those who lose win

1328 Will we sulk and know it again—the taste of us joining
Her forehead glistening

1329 Sulk my bright jewel—and may our night
Of pleading be long

1330 Sulking in love is joy—and joining
Again—joy of joys

A COMMENTARY OF NOTES

PART ONE VIRTUE

I. INTRODUCTION

1. IN PRAISE OF GOD

It has long been customary in Tamil, as in many other Indian languages and traditions, to begin a work with a prayer song. These prayers offer praise to a deity or deities in the hope that the poet may complete the work that he or she has felt called to begin. In the first chapter of the four-chapter introduction to the Tirukkural, Tiruvalluvar gives ten verses that are inclusive enough for commentators of all kinds to have found reflections of their own traditions within them. One may see these qualities as qualities of God, or of particular gods, or of the god-like *tirthankaras*, the spiritual teachers, of Jainism.

Quotation marks indicate a literal translation. Their absence indicates an additional connotation or interpretive note on context. When giving several literal translations for a single word, I repeat the one I've chosen to draw attention to the full array of possibilities one would find consulting a Tamil dictionary. Translations or interpretations separated by a comma indicate synonyms; translations or interpretations separated by a semicolon indicate different and sometimes competing possibilities.

1 *God:* "primordial being," "first mover," "Lord of the Beginning." This kural is usually thought to be about letters: Just as the Tamil alphabet begins with the letter A, so too does the world begin with God. However, the word for "letter" refers even more deeply to the sound that is the basis of speech. As the great Tamil grammarians make clear, language begins with sound, to which we then give written form. The "ah" of breath is the beginning of all sounds and letters; like this, the world begins in that Being which begins.

2 *touching the feet:* worshipping.

3 *At the feet:* "joined to the feet." To be one with; to set one's mind-and-heart upon a god without ceasing.
mind in flower: "he who walks upon flowers," "he who enters the flower of our hearts."

5 *The two deeds that bring darkness:* good deeds and bad deeds, both of which bring confusion.
Both kinds of deeds lead back to the cycle of rebirth. The release that the Kural has as its ultimate aim goes beyond the cycle of good and evil.
God: "God," "Lord," "King."

7 *hard:* that is, impossible.
hearts: heart-and-mind.

8 *compassion:* "virtue," the first of the three parts of the Kural.
the other two: the other great "oceans," wealth and love, the second and third parts of the Kural. All three are realms where a person can drown.

10 *swim the sea of birth:* implicitly, cross to the other side.
God: "God," "Lord," "King."

2. THE GLORY OF RAIN

The order of Tiruvalluvar's chapters offers its own silent commentary, with the glory of rain second only to the glories of divinity.

11 *ambrosia:* as in Greek mythology, the nectar of the gods that yields eternal life.

12 In Tamil, this verse sounds like rain. Here is a rough transliteration:
Tuppaarkku tuppaaya tuppaakki tuppaarkku
Tuppaaya tuuum mazhai

14 *wealth:* natural and continual abundance.

16 *hard:* that is, impossible.

17 *gather:* both in the sense of gathering together and of gathering water from the sea.

18 *below:* on earth.

19 *austerity: tavam,* that virtue or power by which a person achieves a greater form of connection by letting go of some desire. See chapter 27.

20 *flow:* Tiruvalluvar uses the word "flow," *oḻukku,* to refer simul-

taneously to the flowing of water and to the conduct that flows from a person of character.

This image of conduct as akin to water flowing on earth deeply informs Tiruvalluvar's understanding of virtue. In both this translation and its notes, wherever one sees the word "conduct," one should also think of the image of water flowing.

3. THE GREATNESS OF LETTING GO

"The Greatness of Renunciants."

21 *that way / Which is theirs:* The word here for "way," *oḻukkam*, comes from the same root as the word in verse 20 for "flow," *oḻukku*. Just as water flows through the earth, fitting the land that it touches, so too can a human being live in that way that is uniquely their own.

23 *the two:* the cycle of birth and the release from the cycle of birth. Notice that while letting go is clearly great, Tiruvalluvar devotes twenty chapters to the way of the householder and thirteen to the way of renunciation. Many glories may be great.

24 *the five:* the five senses. See kural 27.
The unspoken image is of an elephant that a person guides with a prod.

25 Commentators give different reasons for how Indra bears witness to the power that commands the senses. Some say that he managed to achieve this power and by doing so earned his position as ruler. Others see him instead as a negative example, citing the story of how he seduced Ahalya, the wife of the sage Gautama, and was then cursed by the sage. But perhaps both interpretations are true. The power that commands all five must continue to command all five.

26 *the impossible:* "that which is hard to do," "that which is rare to do."

27 *The world:* In Tiruvalluvar and in Tamil, "the world" also means the community of the learned and wise.

28 *The secret:* words that have power hidden within them, like words spoken by saints.
those of true words: When those of true words speak, what they say happens in the world.

29 *hard:* that is, impossible.

One moment of rage: Even saints who have climbed the great hill of character are subject to human emotion. In the moment between when they first feel anger and when they cool that anger, that anger has extraordinary power.

30 *embody grace:* "are beautiful," "are blessed."

they show / Compassion to all: they move like water that flows, showing grace and compassion to all beings.

4. THE IMPERATIVE OF RIGHT ACTION

Right Action: "virtue," "compassion," "generosity."

31 *A life:* a living being; that part of a body that is alive.

34 *purity:* "the action of becoming free of all taints."

35 *freedom from:* "the happening unstained by."

36 *without waiting:* literally, without saying "we can know and act later."

remains / Beside one: is a companion, an aid, a foundation.

37 *No need to speak of virtue:* literally, no need to say "this is what's right."

who is borne / And who bears: In one interpretation, by right action one attains in another birth the place of the one bearing or the one borne. In another interpretation, right action carries us even after the death of our body.

38 *the way back:* the way back to the cycle of birth and death.

39 *Right action:* Parimēlaḻakar links the right action spoken of in this kural with the home life described in the next twenty chapters.

40 *Action that fits:* action that fits a particular person. It is key that although birth is common to all, the two ways of life that Tiruvalluvar delineates—the householder's and the renunciant's—are distinct. What is virtue to one may be vice to another. Everything hinges on what fits a person and the way of life that is theirs.

II. HOUSEHOLDING

5. THE HOME LIFE

Both the life pertaining to a home and the life of the home itself. Without them, the rest of the world falls apart.

41 *One at home:* often translated as "householder" but as much

about the inner life and orientation of such a figure as about his place in the outer world.
stands in goodness: literally, stands on the way or path of goodness. The word here for "way" can also mean "river."
the three other stations: the student, the one who retires with his wife to the forest, and the renunciant or ascetic.

43 *Nothing is higher:* Here Tiruvalluvar uses the Tamil word for "head" to refer to what stands above all other possibilities. Just as the head is the highest part of the human body, the honoring of these realms is the highest part of human life.
Spirits: forebears, ancestors.

45 *root and flower:* "its nature and its reward."

47 *stands above:* "is head to," "is chief among."

48 *The home life that guides others:* both in the sense of helping others on their way and of being exemplary and unerring in virtue.
guides: helps others flow like water. The verb in Tamil, *oḻukki*, comes from the same root as *oḻukku* in 20 and *oḻukkam* in 21.

50 *thriving in the life at home:* flourishing in the practice of virtue.

6. IN PRAISE OF ONE'S LIFE COMPANION

Although this chapter is concerned with what it means to be a wife, its title places the emphasis on the quality of companionship, leaving the companion's gender unspecified. The qualities described here are qualities we might praise in many kinds of people, depending on the play of circumstance. These verses are simultaneously about husbands and wives, and more than husbands and wives.

51 *greatness:* greatness of character and greatness of action.
husband: literally, "the one who has received one."
Abundance: income, means, fertility, fullness.

54 *fidelity:* another age would render this as "chastity," but "chastity" is too chaste for the power that Tamil and Tiruvalluvar perceive in this quality.

56 *Her husband:* literally, "the one who has received one."
the power of words: the words spoken about her and the words she speaks.

57 *walls:* the image is of the walls of a prison.
safety within: the unwavering firmness and strength of fidelity.
Keeps her safe: is the highest form, the "head," of safety.

7. HAVING CHILDREN

61 *Children with knowledge:* Tiruvalluvar is concerned not simply with the bearing of children but with the way in which knowledge, intelligence, and wisdom are passed down generation by generation.

62 *all seven lives:* according to Parimēlaḻakar, the seven kinds of birth that a life can take: vegetable, reptilian, marine, avian, four-legged, human, and divine. Commentators also interpret this phrase as meaning seven consecutive births through which a single life may pass.

63 *one's deeds:* the deeds of one's parents.

64 *ambrosia:* as in kural 11, the nectar of the gods that yields eternal life.

For those versed in classical Tamil literature, this kural brings to mind the following poem by Pāṇṭiyaṉ Aṟivuṭai Nampi, collected in the anthology *Puṟanāṉūṟu*, which pre-dates the Kural by several centuries:

Even if he makes much and eats with many
Owning great riches if no children
Enter in taking tiny steps stretching little hands
Throwing touching grabbing smearing
Spreading ghee rice all over
Their bodies beguiling all sense
All a man's days mean nothing

66 *babble:* the sweet prattle of young voices discovering the world.

67 *among men:* literally, "in the assembly of the learned."

70 *What did he do to have him:* what austerities did he undertake to be blessed with him.

8. HAVING LOVE

Tamil has many words for love, each with its own flavor and sphere. The love here is the love of family, different from the romantic and erotic love of part III and the impartial love for all beings of the renunciant.

71 *the fullness of one's heart:* including the sense of compassion by which one sees the hardship faced by another.

72 *Bones too:* some commentators take this as a reference to the

sage Dadhichi, said to have offered up his bones to Indra, Lord of the Gods, in a battle between good and evil.

74 *Glory:* the word here also suggests release from the cycle of birth and death.

75 Householders achieve release through the joys of married life; renunciants achieve release through the hardship of austerities.

76 *friend:* companion, support, aid, defense.

77 *a body writhing without bones:* a worm squirming on the ground.

78 Implicitly, without love in one's heart one doesn't live.

79 *what good / Is the eye of a body:* what good are all the outer organs.

9. HOSPITALITY

In Tamil, the word for "hospitality" combines a word for "stranger" or "guest" with a word for "to care for," "to cherish," or "to protect." To offer hospitality is to cherish and protect the stranger who arrives at one's door.

81 *generosity:* the word Tiruvalluvar uses for "generosity" can also mean "the cultivation of soil." Generosity, as both Tamil and English suggest, is rooted in the practice of generation.

82 *nectar of the gods:* "undying medicine," "medicine that keeps one from death."

84 *Prosperity:* Lakshmi, the goddess of prosperity, evoked in the Tamil with an epithet meaning "she who makes everything happen."

85 *who partakes with his guests:* the Tamil offers the sense both that one's guests eat first and that one's guests eat as one eats oneself.

86 *Guests to the gods above:* here "guests" carries the sense of "welcome guests," "good guests," "guests of excellent quality."

87 *it rests / On the nature of each guest:* is proportionate to the goodness of each guest.

88 *who don't dare:* who do not undertake, with the sense of the head—the highest part of the body—leading.

89 *fools:* in the Tamil, the word also suggests miserliness.

90 *Anicham flowers:* flowers said to be exceedingly delicate. *When a face turns sour:* when the face of a host turns sour.

10. SWEET SPEECH

"Saying What Is Sweet." In the Tamil, the phrase isn't burdened with connotations of "sweet talk" or "sweet talking" as in English. To speak what is sweet is to speak without guile.

91 *love:* the Tamil word here also means "wetness," "moisture," and "the coolness of water." Just as good conduct is akin to the way that streams and rivers fit the land through which they flow, love is akin to the life-giving coolness of water.

92 *with a smile:* with one's face blossoming. Even when we feel we have nothing to give, we can give a few sweet words.

93 *right action:* "virtue."

94 *hardship of hunger:* the hardship of not eating, of not being able to feed the senses.

96 *Good:* "virtue."
wrong: "that which is not [good]," "those things which are not [good]."

97 *grant:* yield, grow.
goodness: fruit, benefit.
Without ceasing to be sweet: "without turning from their nature," understood implicitly to be sweet.

98 *Here and hereafter:* in this life and the next.

100 *eating sour:* seizing unripened fruit, still sour and bitter to the tongue.

11. GRATITUDE

Not simply a feeling but the action of remembering the good others have done.

103 Not only is good to be done without reference to past gains but also without reference to future profit.

104 *tree:* literally, a palmyra tree, both imposing in size and eminently useful for its wood, leaves, sap, and fruit.
seed: literally, a tiny millet seed.

105 Compare with kural 87.

106 *Who held:* who was one's strength and support.

107 *Remembered:* implicitly, remembered by those of goodness.
seven births: see the note to kural 62.

108 Remembering afflicts the rememberer, not the wrongdoer.

109 *the worst / Of wrongs:* "wrongs tantamount to murder," "wrongs tantamount to killing."

110 *redemption:* "redemption," "escape."

12. FAIRNESS

To stand in the middle in upright impartiality.

111 *Fairness:* "propriety," "fitness," "fittingness," "excellence."

115 *wisdom:* "the wise," "people of greatness."

117 *decline:* financial decline, poverty.
the wise: "the world." See the note to kural 27.

118 *an impartial mind:* "not bending to one side."

119 *absent:* "entirely absent."

13. SELF-CONTROL

121 *darkness:* "unbearable darkness," "hell."

122 *truth:* "truth," "meaning," "thing," "wealth."

123 *the path of wisdom:* "on the path of knowing knowledge."
glory and renown: recognition and esteem from the wise.

124 *Steady in one's state:* standing firm on the path that is one's own.

125 *the wealthy:* those rich not simply in material means but in learning and family.

126 *all five:* the five senses. See kural 27.
like a tortoise: as a tortoise contains its five limbs.
seven lives: see the note to kural 62.

128 *Even once with harsh words:* this can also be translated "even with one harsh word."

129 *words:* "tongues," "a tongue."

130 The god of virtue arrives on their path at the moment they need it most.

14. THE POSSESSION OF CONDUCT

Conduct: oḻukkam, the way of life that fits each person, as water fits the earth and flows. See also the notes to kurals 20 and 21.

133 *Falls low:* "gains a low birth." As Maṇakkuṭavar puts it: "Even if one is born into a low community, by one's conduct one is high; even if one is born into a high community, by losing conduct one is low."

134 *may be relearned:* if a Brahmin forgets a mantra, he can relearn it without doing harm to his standing and his people.
Destroys his birth: implicitly, he destroys his people and their way of life as well.

140 *flow with:* move in harmony with. See the notes to kurals 20 and 21.

15. FIDELITY

"Not Desiring Another Man's Wife."

143 *more than dead:* though their bodies may be alive, their lives have ended.

144 *The heedless man:* "the one not attending even a millet seed's worth to what he is doing."

147 *A man:* a householder.

148 *virtue:* "virtue to the wise."
fortitude: "great strength," "great manhood," "great mastery."

149 *this earth of fierce waters:* this land encircled by fearsome seas.

150 *evil:* "evil," "wrong," "sin," "vice."

16. FORBEARANCE

151 *digging:* "those who dig."
scorn: "those who scorn."

152 *forget it:* forget it at once. See also kural 108.

154 *excellence:* "excellence," "perfection," "integrity," "fullness of character."

157 *wrong:* "that which is not fitting."

158 *arrogant insolence:* transgressions arising from transgression.
Inborn patience: forbearance, with the additional sense of fitting what is great and true.

159 *saints:* renouncers.
Vicious mouths: "the bitter words of impudent mouths."

160 *harsh words:* "the bitter words spoken by others."

17. FREEDOM FROM ENVY

161 *way:* "path," "river."
virtue: conduct. Tiruvalluvar uses the same word here as in kural 20, *oḻukku*. The way of virtue is like a flowing river.
freedom / From: "the nature of not having," "the quality of not having."

166 *family:* "those surrounding," "those encircling."
167 *Fortune:* Lakshmi, the goddess of wealth.
her wayward sister: Lakshmi's older sister, the goddess of misfortune.
168 *the fire:* hell.

18. FREEDOM FROM GREED

171 *good things:* life's necessities, what's needed for virtue.
172 *wrong:* "that which is censured."
bias: "lack of fairness."
173 *wrong:* "that which is not virtuous."
another pleasure: the unending delight that comes from virtue.
174 *see:* "see without fault," "see without distortion."
175 *great learning:* "fine and expansive knowledge."
176 *the seeker of grace:* one on the path of virtue seeking grace.
179 *fortune:* Lakshmi, the goddess of wealth.
embraces: "joins with."

19. FREEDOM FROM BACKBITING

"Not Speaking Behind," "Not Speaking Outside."

182 *cursing:* defying, flouting, blaspheming.
184 *speaking evil:* "speaking what's not kind," "speaking what's not compassionate," "cutting one's own eye by one's talk."
forgetting what follows: forgetting consequences.
185 *Vile and backbiting words:* "baseness that bites backs."
hearts / That speak no virtue: implicitly, mouths that pretend goodness.
187 *with their words:* with backbiting words.
speak joyfully and make friends: enjoy true friendship. Tiruvalluvar's comment on Iago a millennium before Shakespeare wrote *Othello.*
190 *soul:* "life that endures."

20. FREEDOM FROM FRUITLESS SPEECH

191 *many:* implicitly, an assembly of the wise.
194 *denatured words:* words without quality or character.
an assembly: an assembly of the wise.
196 *husk:* "husk," "chaff."

197 *without goodness:* "without goodness," "without justice," "without excellence," "without heart."

198 *the highest fruit:* salvation, release.

21. FEAR OF WRONGDOING

201 *fear:* dread.
confusion: "confusion," "arrogance," or the arrogance that comes from confusion. Commentators often speak of this state as a kind of intoxication.

202 In the Tamil, Tiruvalluvar plays on the similarities between the words for "wrong" and "fire." Both come from the same root, which suggests that wrongdoing, like a fire, can burn the one who starts it and spiral easily out of control. Unlike fire, however, the consequences of wrongdoing can appear far removed in time and space.

204 *when forgetful:* accidentally, inadvertently.
virtue: the god of virtue.
means harm / To: this can also be translated as "renounces," for in the absence of virtue, harm comes of a course.

205 *again and again:* implicitly, in this life and the next.

208 *Like a shadow underfoot:* just as a shadow remains beneath the person who casts it.

209 *think:* the word in Tamil conveys the sense of "approach with the mind."

22. KNOWING WHAT IS FITTING

A particularly Tamil idea, not found in the same way in the Sanskrit Vedas.

211 *Kindness:* being true to the nature—to the kind—of oneself and others.

212 *being generous:* "generosity," "the cultivation of soil." See the note to kural 81.

214 *know kindness:* know and live in accordance with the nature of the world.

215 *well:* literally, a body of water that serves a place where people dwell, as in a reservoir or village tank.
Who love the world: who love the people; who enact their love for the nature of the world.

216 *good people:* people of grace, people of goodness, people who practice kindness. Contrast with kural 1008.

217 *A tree granting remedies:* a tree whose every part becomes medicine.

great people: people of great quality and virtue. Contrast with kural 1008.

219 *way:* "way," "path," "river."

what is fitting: that which is worth doing. In the Tamil, the word for this quality evokes as well the word for water.

220 *generosity:* doing what is fitting.

23. GIVING

Chapters 22, 23, and 24 form a trio on different aspects of generosity. Parimēlaḻakar notes that while chapter 22 places the accent on this life, this chapter places the accent on the next.

221 *Giving:* "giving one thing." Giving the thing that is needed.

223 *Giving:* giving to those who cry, "I have nothing."

225 *the strong:* ascetics who have mastered their senses.

226 *ruinous hunger:* hunger that destroys a person's goodness.

227 *vicious:* "evil," "fiery."

228 *The joy of giving:* both to the one giving and the one receiving.

24. RENOWN

This chapter brings the section on householding to a close with the renown on earth that comes of generosity in a settled and upright life.

232 *giving what's needed:* "giving to those who ask."

those / Who speak: implicitly, the wise.

236 *appear:* appear in this world, come into this world, be born as a human being in this world.

238 *Leaving a name:* as one leaves a legacy or progeny in the world.

239 *Beneath:* beneath the weight of.

240 *without name:* without inviting renown.

Without blame: without incurring blame.

III. RENUNCIATION

25. COMPASSION

The compassion of saints and ascetics. Parimēlaḻakar divides section III into two subsections, placing chapters 25–33 under the heading of "vows," "fasting," or "religious practice."

242 *it alone:* literally, "even if you examine [other paths], it alone."
Sees one to the end: "is companion."
of every path: of the many paths of different faiths and traditions.

243 *knows:* "has joined with."

245 *world:* implicitly, the good people of this world.

246 *lose everything but disdain:* "lose everything and forget." Implicitly, lose virtue and fall into forgetfulness that ends in disdain.

247 *No heaven without compassion:* "that world is not for those without compassion."
no earth / Without wealth: "this world is not for those without wealth."
wealth: "things," "possessions," "meaning," "substance."

249 *without wisdom:* "without clarity."

250 *Before those weaker:* implicitly, when you come in anger before those weaker.

26. REFUSING MEAT

Refusing meat as a principle for renunciants.

252 *care:* protection, defense, safeguarding.

253 *hearts:* "hearts," "chests," "minds."
no grace: no turning toward goodness.
minds: "minds," "hearts."

254 *virtue:* goodness, meaning, sense.

255 *lies:* endures.

259 *fire:* sacrificial fire.

27. TAVAM

Austerities endured. The word comes from the Sanskrit word *tapas*, which also means "heat." Tavam is the energy generated by acts of austerity.

261 *form:* body, shape, figure.

262 Unless it is already part of one's nature, one's tavam will be an empty gesture. One's actions, however, can lead to its possibility and cultivation.

263 *the others:* householders.

A key to this verse is the word "wanting." Although giving is no doubt good, those who've let go have no need to be given to. They've gone beyond needing and not needing. That is why their tavam leads to release. Householders who desire to do something good are still attached to desire. But if they do their duty to be doing their duty, not in order to gain anything else, they too remember tavam—that tavam which is theirs to do.

264 *if:* implicitly, one with tavam would not think these things.

265 *in this life:* According to Parimēlaḻakar, "in this life" implies that what the renunciant seeks corresponds to the next life.

266 *their duty:* that which fits their station in life.

267 *Affliction:* "the burning and burning of affliction."

268 *Those whose lives aren't their own:* those beyond "me" and "mine." This can also be translated, "Those who've attained mastery over their own lives."

269 *attain:* "to join heads with."

In this verse, there is a striking juxtaposition of the words for "head" and "hand," as if to suggest that achieving tavam with the highest part of one's body brings all possibilities to one's hands.

28. UNWORTHY CONDUCT

"Conduct That Is Not Fitting," "Conduct That Does Not Match." Here, the conduct in question is conduct that does not fit tavam and the way of renunciation.

271 *heart:* heart-and-mind.

within: Even if others, without, believe one's false conduct, the five senses within do not.

272 *To tower to the sky:* to appear to have a stellar reputation.

273 *command:* strength, self-control.

274 *wrong:* "what is not tavam."

275 *make him cry out:* "make him suffer and cry out."

276 *living by falsehood:* living off others.

277 *red rosary pea: Abrus precatorius.* A single pea ingested can kill a person.

278 *Plunging into the waters of greatness:* bathing and behaving like saints.

280 *the wise:* "the world." See the note to kural 27.
shave: shave one's head.

29. FREEDOM FROM STEALING

Stealing: "stealing," "deception."

281 *heart:* heart-and-mind.

282 *Even the thought:* "even thinking the thought with one's heart-and-mind."
thieve: "take by stealth."

283 *by stealth:* "by stealth," "by stealing."
Declines utterly: including whatever virtue one has gained.

284 *in the end:* "in the ripening," "in consequence."

285 *lapse:* lapse in another's attention. The sense is of thieves who watch for their chance.

286 *fit:* correspond to and embody, as water fits the land through which it flows. See the notes to chapter 14 and to kurals 20 and 21.
what fits: grace, measure, proportion, goodness.

287 *darkness:* "the dark knowledge."
those knowing: "those who aspired to and have gained."
grace: proportion, measure, goodness.

288 *loves:* "knows."
grace: proportion, measure, goodness.
deception / In: "deception abides in."

289 *err:* "do what is not good," "do what is not fitting," "do what is out of proportion."

290 *Heaven:* "the world of the gods."
life: here a phrase that could mean either "life that endures" or "the seat of life." Maṇakkuṭavar interprets this as release itself. Parimēlaḻakar, on the other hand, interprets it as one's body, yielding the sense "even bodies fail those who steal."

30. TRUTH

294 *lives / Without:* "learns to conduct oneself without," "learns to flow in action without."

295 *stands above:* like the head above the body.
generosity and tavam: "those who enact generosity and tavam."
298 *without: puṟam.* In classical Tamil poetry, one of two main spheres of poetry and experience. *Puṟam* refers to the outer world of politics, economy, and war.
within: akam. In classical Tamil poetry, the other main sphere of poetry and experience. *Akam* refers to the inner world of the heart.
300 *truer:* "better," "greater," "more splendid."

31. FREEDOM FROM ANGER

301 *guard:* watch, restrain, protect.
has sway: as with those weaker than oneself.
303 *Bear anger toward none:* "forget anger with everyone."
304 *joy and laughter:* Here we can see the distinction between the inner, *akam*, and the outer, *puṟam*. Joy is known inside; laughter appears outside. See also the note to kural 298.
306 *one's teachers:* "one's community," "one's friends," "one's associates." All those able to help one cross the sea of birth.
307 *power:* substance, thing, meaning.
308 *scorched:* "wronged as if scorched."
310 *sail beyond:* "renounce," "let go of."

32. DOING NO HARM

Harm: "unsweetness."

311 *Even for:* "even if one could get." Implicitly, such wealth cannot actually be had, since any apparent glory would be flawed.
312 *striking:* harming.
314 *wrongdoers:* "those who do harm."
release them: forgot both their act and one's own.
315 *see:* consider, understand, regard.
316 *recognized:* understood, realized, experienced, felt.
317 *Highest of all:* "chief," "head."
anywhere: "anytime."
318 *the lives of others:* "lives that endure."
320 *pain:* "all pain," "all harm," "all sorrow," "all illness."

33. FREEDOM FROM KILLING

322 *authors:* authorities on ethics.
life: "many lives," "all lives," "all beings."
stands highest: as the head above the body.

324 *a good way:* "a good way," "the good way," "the right way." The word here for "way" also means "river."

325 *stasis:* the state of being stuck in the round of rebirth.

326 *Life-ending:* "life-eating."

327 *sweet life:* dear life.

328 *Does not suit:* "is last," "is least," "is lowest."
gained by virtue: Parimēlaḻakar interprets this to mean the wealth gained by the householder through sacrifices to the gods.

34. IMPERMANENCE

For Parimēlaḻakar, this chapter begins the second subsection within renunciation, chapters 34–37, "wisdom."

336 *Here yesterday gone today:* "the man who was yesterday is not today."

337 *think millions on millions of thoughts:* plan millions and millions of things.

340 *sheltered:* resting, snuggled.
Home: "dwelling that one can enter."

35. RENUNCIATION

As both Parimēlaḻakar and Maṇakkuṭavar note in their commentaries, what one renounces is attachment. Even living in a body and related to other things, the person who grasps nothing is free.

341 For Parimēlaḻakar, the repetition in this verse indicates multiplicity. One must let go of many, many things, whether all at once or one thing at a time.

342 *All that delights:* all that yields delight by being right and fitting.

346 *beyond gods:* "higher than the gods can reach."

348 *touch heaven:* "attain the head," "reach what is highest."
Fall: "succumb to delusion."

36. KNOWING WHAT IS REAL

What Is Real: "truth," "reality," "soul," "consciousness," "body."

351 *Delusion:* "delusion," "confusion," "ignorance."

birth without light: "birth without greatness," "birth without splendor."

352 *delusion:* "delusion," "confusion," "ignorance."
glory: "joy," "bliss." By extension, "freedom," "release."

353 *delusion:* here, "doubt," "uncertainty."

355 *kind:* nature, quality, property.

356 *here:* in this world.
reach: "attain the head," "reach what is highest."
The path beyond here: "the path that does not return here."

359 *severs all bonds:* "conducts oneself so that all bonds sever."

37. SEVERING FROM DESIRE

364 *Purity:* implicitly, salvation, release from the cycle of birth.

365 *Those beyond desire:* "those who have severed from desire."
are beyond: "are said [by the wise] to have severed."

366 *fearing:* dreading, guarding against.

367 *happen:* "come."
as hoped: "in the way one desires," "in the way one seeks." The word here for "way" also means "river."

370 *in that moment:* in that state, then and there.

IV. FATE

38. FATE

The last chapter of part 1 and the only chapter in the Tirukkural to have a section of its own.

371 *wealth:* "wealth at hand." Implicitly, "wealth that aids," "wealth that is available for use."

373 *Innate knowledge:* as determined by fate.

374 *two:* The fate that brings wisdom is different than the fate that brings wealth.

375 *When gaining:* "in gaining wealth," "in making wealth."
all bad becomes good: all once unfavorable becomes favorable.
All good becomes bad: all once favorable becomes unfavorable.
Both changes are changes in fate.

378 *would go without:* would renounce. Since fate exempts no one, those with nothing seek to escape by having, not by renouncing. Implicitly, renunciation itself comes by fate.

380 Nonetheless, see also kural 620.

PART TWO WEALTH

This word, like this part of Tiruvalluvar's book, encompasses a wide range of human experience. Its root meaning is "thing," "matter," or "entity" but extends to meanings such as "meaning," "subject," "learning," and "wealth." See also chapter 76.

The seventy chapters of part II fall into three sections: sovereignty (kurals 39–63), the arms of government (kurals 64–95), and other matters pertaining to politics and worldly life (96–108).

I. SOVEREIGNTY

39. THE SPLENDOR OF KINGS

"The Splendor of Kings," "Splendor for Kings." The qualities that make a true leader.

381 *kingdom:* "family," "people," "community," including the land itself.
highest: the word here also means "bull" or "lion."
382 *energy:* diligence, enterprise, drive.
in fullness: "without deficiency."
384 *honor:* "the honor of bravery," "the honor of valor."
385 *makes:* "creates possibility."
assigns: allots, apportions, distributes.
386 *easy to approach:* "easily seen."
387 *who cares / And gives:* "who is strong enough to care and give."
389 *bears:* withstands.
bitter words: Parimēlaḻakar reads this as the harsh but true words of a king's advisors. See kurals 447 and 448.
390 *kindness:* graciousness, compassion.
vigilance: watchful of the people's welfare.

40. LEARNING

That learning which pertains to a leader.

391 *Faultlessly study:* study till all questions and uncertainties have been cleared.
fit: fit oneself to, live in accordance with.
392 *lives with life:* living beings, living souls.
Just as two eyes provide a single vision with depth, so too do numbers and letters provide a clear view of the whole.

394 *work:* labor, profession.
meeting: as clouds join together to shower rain.

395 *the poor:* "those without."
the rich: "those with."
The learned bow in humility before those who are rich in learning and thus continue to learn; those without such humility will always be low, no matter their outward standing.

396 *well:* "a well in sand," "a well in sandy soil."
fills: springs forth water.
learns: the word in Tamil implies digging, sharing its form with a word meaning "stone," "rock," or "gem."
a mind deepens: "springs forth knowledge."

398 *safeguard:* security, support, aid.
all seven lives: see the note to kural 62.

399 *When the world takes delight:* "when they see the world delighting."
love: love of learning.

400 One can see this kural as a commentary on all the other kurals about wealth. Tiruvalluvar's book is not so much a collection as it is a constellation.

41. LACK OF LEARNING

401 *books:* "noble books," "books of fullness," "books that are full."

402 *without breasts:* "without two breasts," "without both breasts."
womanhood: womanliness, maidenhood, maidenliness.

408 *the good:* good people; people of knowledge.
When the learned meet poverty, that poverty does not ruin them. When the unlearned meet wealth, everyone suffers.

409 *born high:* born into a family of high rank.
born low: born into a family of low rank.

42. LISTENING

The capacity to receive knowledge and wisdom from the words of others.

411 *Riches of the ear:* the knowledge one gains by listening to wise elders.
highest: "head," "chief."

412 *When the ear:* implicitly, only when the ear.

a little: as Parimēlaḻakar notes, too much given to the belly leads to discomfort and illness. The same is not true of the wisdom one hears.

413 *Fed through their fire:* "fed by offerings," offered through fire. See also kural 259.

414 *holds one up:* "is a companion that supports one," "is an aid that supports one."

415 *the virtuous:* "those who possess conduct."

417 *listen deeply:* "listen and reflect deeply."

418 *entered them:* "penetrated one's ears."

419 *hard:* that is, impossible.
to be humble: to bow down, as in prayer. The phrase implies both humility of speech and humility of conduct.

420 As Maṇakkuṭavar puts it, "What harm comes if they die, and what good if they live?"

43. THE POSSESSION OF KNOWLEDGE

Intelligence, wisdom, perception, learning.

421 *that falls to no enemy:* "that falls to no enemy," "that no enemy can enter."

422 *keeps the mind steady:* "keeps it from roaming where it roams." Parimēlaḻakar interprets this as the capacity of the mind not to dwell in the senses, not to go where the senses may go.

423 *discerning / Its truth:* "seeing its true substance," "seeing its true meaning."

425 *the wise:* "the world." See the note to kural 27.
not blooming / And then drooping: being constant, unlike a flower that blossoms and then wilts.

426 *the great:* "the world." See the note to kural 27.

427 *foresee:* "know what comes," "know what becomes."

428 *work:* labor, profession.
knowing: "those who know."

430 *Having all:* "whatever they may have."

44. ELIMINATION OF FAULTS

Elimination of those faults that are not only detrimental in a leader but to which any leader may be particularly prone.

431 *depravity:* "smallness." Commentators traditionally interpret this as "lust."

432 *arrogance:* "pride without goodness."

433 *seed:* "millet seed."
tree: "palmyra tree."
The same pairing appears in kural 104.

434 *treasure:* wealth, substance, meaning.

435 *guard beforehand:* implicitly, guard against faults.

436 *fault*: flaw, error, distress.

437 *do their duty:* "do what needs doing."

438 *Unlike any other:* "not one to be counted among any others."

439 *acclaim oneself:* be amazed at oneself.
What: any deed that.

45. GAINING THE HELP OF THE GREAT

Maṇakkuṭavar explains this as "gaining the help of those whose knowledge is more mature than one's own." To be a king or leader of any kind, one must surround oneself with men and women of the highest caliber.

441 *study / And gain:* "know their qualities, select, and gain."

443 *As one's own:* as one's family, as one's closest associates.

444 *Moving with:* moving with as water moves. The word has the same root as "conduct."

445 *Counselors are eyes:* "one conducts oneself with counselors as one's eyes."

446 *right:* good, fitting, worthy.

447 *thunder:* reprove, rebuke, censure.

448 *thunders:* is able to reprove, rebuke, and censure.

449 *without principal:* "for one without principal."
permanence: stability, standing.
Without pillars: "for one without pillars."

450 *earning foes:* "earning many foes."

46. FREEDOM FROM SMALLNESS

"Not Joining with Those Who Are Small," "Not Fitting Oneself to Small-Minded Companions."

451 *smallness:* not of size, but of mind; baseness.
company: family, kindred.

452 *nature:* "nature," "quality," "character."

what we know: one's knowledge, one's intelligence.
See kural 1323 for another image of land and water being changed in joining.

453 *knowledge:* perception, the capacity to know.

454 *Knowledge:* one's intelligence.
appears of: seems to come from, seems to arise from.

455 *rest / On:* depend upon, are upheld by.

456 *bestows goodness:* "leaves behind what is good," with "what is good" often glossed as "children" or "legacy."
Nothing that fails: "no action that does not turn out good."

457 *all life:* "life that endures," "living beings."

459 *good birth:* "the next life," "joy in the next life" (Parimēlaḻakar), "reward in the next life" (Maṇakkuṭavar).

460 *bad:* evil. The word in Tamil also means "fire," suggesting that bad company can burn.

47. CLARITY BEFORE ACTION

461 *act:* including not acting when not acting is needed.

462 *with clear counsel*: who deliberate with carefully chosen counselors.

463 *possibility:* "capital," "principal," "cause," "root," "foundation."

465 *rise up:* "rise up," "rise upon," "attack."

466 *what is unworthy:* "what is not fit to be done."
What is worthy: "what is fit to be done."

468 *many who care:* many who support, many who guard against failure.

469 *character:* quality, nature.

48. KNOWING STRENGTH

471 *power:* "power," "strength."

472 *deed:* "movement," "movement upon," as in moving on an enemy.

474 *fit:* conduct oneself in accord with.
flaunting / Himself: "being amazed with himself." See kural 439.

476 *keeps climbing:* "knows it and keeps climbing."

477 *Give rightly knowing one's limits:* "know one's limits and give in the proper way," "know one's limits and give in the proper channel," "know the limits of the river and give."

478 *earning:* "the channel of increase," "the river of becoming."

spending: "the channel of decrease," "the river of going."
479 *appears full:* "seems to exist."
falls completely: "becomes nothing with no way to appear again."
480 *Generosity:* "what is fitting." See chapter 22.

49. KNOWING TIME

481 *need time:* must know the right time for action.
486 *strength:* energy, drive.
488 *enemies:* enemies with force, mighty enemies.
490 We find the same image seven centuries later in Avvaiyar's *The Word That Endures*:

> *Don't think to conquer the one who holds back,*
> *Concluding he must lack sense.*
> *Perched on the sluicegate*
> *Letting the running fish run, the white crane*
> *Waits for the catch.*
>
> from *Give, Eat, and Live: Poems of Avvaiyar*

50. KNOWING PLACE

492 *a fortress:* one's own or that of another's.
493 *opponents:* "those who do not protect."
494 *friends:* "those fitted together," "those close."
in force: with minds fitted together, with thoughts closely aligned. From the same root as the word here for "friends."
497 *omits nothing:* omits nothing in thinking.
498 *a small place:* "a place fit for the leader of small armies."
greatness: "greatness," "force," "energy," "drive."
500 *The elephant . . . without fear:* "the elephant whose eyes fear nothing."
foes: "spear-men."

51. KNOWING AND TRUSTING

Attaining clarity about and trusting those worthy to be trusted.

501 *Virtue wealth pleasure:* also the three parts of the Tirukkural.
pleasure: one's understanding of and relationship to pleasure.
awe: fear and reverential wonder at life and death.
these four / In depth: "the quality of these four."

a king chooses: "are chosen," "must be chosen." Implicitly, ministers are chosen, ministers must be chosen.

502 *free of faults:* having removed oneself from faults.
unwilling to risk shame: shrinking from the shame of wrongdoing.

504 *Take what is greatest:* select those in whom character outweighs faults most greatly.

506 *Trust no one:* "guard against trusting anyone."
without ties: without family (Parimēlaḻakar), without conduct (Maṇakkuṭavar).

507 *fond trust:* trusting only on the basis of fondness.

508 *trouble:* "unending trouble," "inexhaustible trouble."

52. KNOWING AND ENGAGING

511 *Seeks:* desires, dwells in, brings forth.

512 *fosters fecundity:* increases natural fertility and abundance.
increases increase: increases revenue.
engage: engage in action, allow to serve.

515 *endure action:* persevere in action.

519 *one:* "the allegiance of one," "the friendship of one," "the liberties of one."
freely: taking the liberties that friendship, trust, and knowledge bestow. That capacity to listen which is the basis of relatedness and kindness.
fully in action: "those acting in action." Those fully engaged in their work.

53. KINDNESS TO KINDRED

521 *kin:* kindred, the circle of one's family and relations.
Ties over time: enduring relatedness.

522 *If one has:* "if it happens that one has."
Wealth that flourishes: "many kinds of wealth that never cease to flourish."

523 *moving:* intermingling, joining with one's heart.

524 *family:* kindred, the circle of one's family and relations.
Flowing freely: moving easily, as water flows.

525 *family:* kindred, the circle of one's family and relations.

527 *call and eat:* call and eat together, call and share food.
those: only those.

528 *Thrive in his sight:* "look to it and live," "look to it and thrive."
530 *and welcome:* implicitly, if the study and reflection show the cause to be suspect, the king shouldn't extend his welcome.

54. ABSENCE OF MIND

531 *neglect:* "negligence," "slackness."
532 *having / To fill daily:* always having to fill one's belly by begging; poverty.
534 *stronghold:* castle, fortress, protection.
refuge: "that which is good." By extension, "abundance," "beauty," "health," "stability," "welfare."
535 *fail:* forget, neglect, slip into negligence.
536 *falls:* slips, neglects by forgetting.
537 *with:* "with the tool of."
538 *do:* "honor and act."
even seven births / Cannot atone: "there is not even in seven births," "there is not even seven births." Parimēlaḻakar and Maṇakkuṭavar take this as meaning "one has no goodness for seven births."
not doing: "neglecting and not doing," "disdaining and not doing."
540 *keeps thinking:* "is able to keep one's thoughts in mind."

55. GOOD RULE

Rule: from the word for "scepter," which in Tamil includes both the rod itself and a sense of goodness, fairness, and rectitude.

541 *Regal with all:* impartial with all people.
clear-eyed: without bias in one's vision.
542 *sky:* implicitly, rain.
the justice of a king: "a king's rule," "a king's scepter."
Parimēlaḻakar: Even if the people have food, without justice it does no good.
543 *the books of priests:* the Vedas.
rest / On: "start from and stand on."
544 *great kings:* "kings of great lands."
545 *abound:* "align," "are in harmony."
546 *bend:* fall prey to partiality.
547 *the world:* "all the world."

548 *who sees no one:* "who cannot easily be seen."
549 *task:* "task," "work," "labor."
550 *Iniquity:* "those who do horrors."
This verse may seem particularly harsh, especially juxtaposed against "Freedom from Killing." What fits the king does not fit the saint. In the next chapter, Tiruvalluvar continues exploring the topic of "iniquity" but as applied to kings, not subjects. This verse thus serves as a hinge between the duties of good rule and the horrors of rule gone awry.

56. HARSH RULE

Rule that "bends" or "goes astray." The word here for "harsh" shares the same root as the word for "iniquity" in kural 550. The line between justice and injustice in a king may be very fine indeed.

551 *torment:* torment their subjects.
accustomed to wrong: "conduct themselves doing wrong."
552 *demanding with a spear:* "like standing with a spear and saying give."
begging: asking one's people for gifts.
555 *the hopeless:* "the helpless who suffer."
force: "force," "army," "tool," "weapon."
556 *light:* renown.
560 *the learned:* priests, Brahmins.

57. STRIKING NO FEAR

561 *what is fitting:* what is proper in response to injustice.
correcting: punishing justly.
Completely: so that the injustice in question does not occur again.
562 *wield:* raise one's weapon to strike.
discharge: cast, hurl, launch.
563 *feared for his deeds:* "whose conduct leads to fearfulness," "whose conduct leads to terror."
564 *crumbles:* "his dwelling diminishes," "his lifespan shrinks."
565 *A ghost seems to hold his riches:* His wealth is useless to himself and others because no one wishes to stand beside him.
566 *lacks eyes:* lacks compassion. See the next chapter, "Eyes That Are Moved."

567 *mettle:* capacity to overcome enemies.
569 *safety:* security, protection, defense.
570 *brings:* "brings," "binds."

58. EYES THAT ARE MOVED

The mercy and compassion of kings. The title of the chapter combines the word for "eye" with a word that means "movement," "flowing," "running," or "current."

571 *beauty:* "beauty," "beautiful woman."
of: "that is," "that is called."
572 *has being:* moves, has nature, abides.
without it / Men: "those without it." Implicitly, kings without it.
574 *appearing:* "seeming to exist," "seeming to be."
in measure: in just proportion.
576 *trees that are stuck in the ground:* Maṇakkuṭavar interprets this phrase to mean "dolls made of wood and mud."
577 *lacks movement:* "lacks eyes that are moved."
578 *The virtuous king:* "the strong who never fail to do right."
579 *in those:* "even in those."
Nothing stands higher: "head."
580 *the poured poison:* Parimēlaḻakar interprets this as "the poison poured by familiars."
kindness: implicitly, the capacity of eyes to be moved.

59. ESPIONAGE

Following "Eyes That Are Moved," another kind of seeing.

581 *conscience:* morals, justice, goodness.
582 *work:* labor, task, profession.
583 *without spies:* "not spying with spies."
seeing what's true: seeing the import of what spies would tell.
584 *those acting:* those acting on behalf of the king.
those near: those around the king, the king's family. Parimēlaḻakar includes the king himself in this circle.
those far: enemies.
586 *cross:* "go past," as in going past a border.
ascetic: renouncer.
yield / To nothing: never flagging in keeping secrets, no matter what others may do.

60. HAVING ENERGY

591 *energy:* the energy and enthusiasm for action.

592 *volition:* the energy of mind, the energy of thought and resolve.

593 *have energy:* "have energy steadily."
at hand: see also the note to kural 371.

596 *thought:* "all thought."
Unachieved: "having failed."
it achieves: "is of the nature of not having failed."

597 *slacken:* become disheartened.

599 *elephant immense and sharp-tusked:* one with strength and with means but without the energy for action.

600 *Strength within:* sturdiness.
are trees not men: are trees that appear as men. Parimēlaḻakar notes that while trees lack the knowledge and capacity for action that belong to humans, men who are like trees cannot bring forth the good things that an actual tree can. Being a tree, in other words, is not the problem. The problem is not being fully what and who one is.

61. FREEDOM FROM SLOTH

601 *sloth:* "the darkness that is sloth."

602 *rise as family:* rise and prosper as a family of renown.
Proceeds: "conducts oneself."

603 *His family:* "the family that gave him birth."
With: "who conducts himself with."

604 *strive:* "strive greatly," "strive for great things."

605 *vessel:* "these four form the vessel," "these four form the boat."

606 *Even with land:* even ruling land.
nothing great: "no fruit that is great."

607 *thunder:* thundering rebuke. See kurals 447 and 448.
strive: "strive greatly."

608 *One:* implicitly, a king.

610 *him who measured the worlds:* the god known as Trivikrama or Vamana who regained the universe from the demon king Bali by measuring it with three steps of his feet.

62. MASTERY OF ACTION

612 *the world:* the community of the learned and wise. See also the note to kural 27.

613 *Generosity:* "generosity," "the cultivation of soil."
614 *energy:* "the command of energy."
615 *seeks:* loves.
family: "one's relatives," "one's kin."
617 *Misfortune:* Lakshmi's older sister, the goddess of misfortune. These sisters also appear in kural 167.
sloth: the word in Tamil can also mean "waist," as if to place the goddess of misfortune in the lap of the slothful.
fortune: Lakshmi, the goddess of wealth, "the one of the lotus."
flower: lotus.
energy: "the energy of one without sloth." The phrase can also be read as "the feet of one without sloth," as if to suggest that fortune comes to the feet of those striving.
618 *luck:* fortune, fate, destiny.
having knowledge: "knowing knowledge," knowing what one should know.
619 *fate:* destiny, the gods.
620 *See the defeat of fate:* "see the backside even of fate." Compare with kural 380.

63. NOT BEING DEFEATED BY ADVERSITY

621 *Triumphs:* "routs it," "overcomes it," "drives it away."
622 *the flood / Of adversity:* "flood-like adversity."
vanishes: comes to ruin.
625 *by its waves:* "even if it comes one upon another."
626 *grasp*: grasp, hoard.
629 *seeking:* "seeking," "desiring."

II. THE ARMS OF GOVERNMENT

64. MINISTERS

This kural opens the second section of part II, "The Arms of Government," kurals 64–95. Maṇakkuṭavar further divides this section into several subsections, the first being "Ministers," kurals 64–73.

631 *action:* "great deeds," "rare action."
632 *protection:* "protection of the people."
Perseverance: "mastery of action."
633 *divide:* create divisions among enemies.

reunite: restore relations with those who have broken away.
cherish and keep: cherish and nurture one's friendships and alliances.

636 *subtlety:* subtlety of an enemy.
last: stand.

637 *action:* the ways of action.

638 *kills knowledge:* strikes down what one who knows says.

65. STRENGTH IN SPEECH

641 *Excellence:* goodness, strength, quality.

642 *weakness:* moral slackness.

643 *those listening:* friends, allies.
those / Not listening: enemies, opponents.

644 *victory:* "wealth." Achievement, attainment.
qualities: one's own qualities and the qualities of those listening (Parimēlaḻakar); the qualities of words (Maṇakkuṭavar).

645 *knowing:* only once one knows.
better: defeat, refute.

646 *Growing love:* growing the desire to keep listening.

647 *hard:* that is, impossible.

649 *who can't:* who lack the clarity to.

650 *learning:* "what they have learned," "what they have studied."

66. PURITY OF ACTION

Purity: faultlessness, truthfulness, holiness.

651 *True allies:* excellence of allies, goodness of allies.
true action: excellence of action, goodness of action.

652 *Shun:* "shun," "renounce."
bears: "bears," "yields," "renders."

653 *light:* one's present renown.
keep becoming: become great.

654 *disgraceful:* "disgraceful," "scornful," "wretched."

655 *regret:* "grieve saying 'what have I done?' "
Do not regret it: "it is better not to regret it." Implicitly, remedy one's actions, rather than waste time wailing.

657 *far above:* "head," "is head to."

658 *Succeeding:* completing those actions spurned by the wise.

659 *Goodness:* "that which is good," "actions that are good."

in time: "after," "afterward."
Maṇakkuṭavar: "All things gained by making others cry make ourselves cry."

660 *an unfired pot:* "a pot made of fresh clay."

67. FIRMNESS OF ACTION

Firmness: resolution.

661 *Firmness of action:* "what is called firmness of action."
firmness of mind: "one's firmness of mind."

663 *misery:* "unending misery."

664 *hard:* rare, great.

665 *inspires the whole:* is acclaimed by all, is respected by all.

666 *steadfast:* steadfast in mind, steadfast in action.

667 *pin:* "axle pin."

670 *when firm:* when otherwise firm.
be prized: "be prized by the world."

68. WAYS OF ACTION

674 *like remnants of fire:* like coals.

675 *out of darkness:* beyond confusion and doubt.

678 *A bull elephant:* "an elephant with wet cheeks," indicating the secretion that appears on a male elephant's cheeks during the period called *musth* when testosterone increases and the elephant's behavior becomes aggressive.

679 *The sideless:* also interpreted as "enemies." Literally, "those not united," those not joined with or to others or oneself.

680 *small places:* small kingdoms.
aware of: "alert to," "fearful of."
yield to: submit to, incline to, seek the help of.

69. DIPLOMACY

681 *good lineage:* long-standing lineage, long-standing nativity to a place.

682 *strength in speaking true:* the capacity to listen and then speak, fitting one's speech to circumstance.

683 *those:* "the nature of those who speak action," the nature of diplomats, the nature of ambassadors.
conquerors: "those bearing weapons." Other kings.

684 *Wisdom:* natural wisdom, innate intelligence.
appearance: "shape," "form," "figure," "grace."

686 *able to convey:* able to drive a matter home.
perceiving / Each moment: able to see what may grant victory in any moment.

687 *Highest of all:* "head."
what is needed: what duty requires.

688 *A true envoy:* "the nature of an envoy," "the nature of one who delivers with words."

689 *The fearless:* the strong of heart.

70. MOVING WITH KINGS

691 *move:* conduct oneself in relation to.

693 *misdeeds:* egregious failings. From the same root—"rare," "difficult," "choice"—as the word translated as "hard."
guards: guards against error, protects oneself.
hard: "hard for anyone," "not possible for anyone."

694 *royalty:* "greatness," "distinction."
desist: "conduct oneself to avoid."

696 *Take note:* take note of the king's moods.
wait: wait for the right time.
What wants to be said: what is gainful for the king to be said.

697 *Speak what is gainful:* speak what is gainful, even if the king doesn't listen (Parimēlaḻakar).
Even when asked: even if pressed by the king.

698 *move:* conduct oneself in relation to.
light: splendor, greatness, divinity.
that's here: that is the king's own.

700 *unkindness:* that which is unseemly, that which is not true to kind.
old friendship: long-standing friendship, generations of relatedness.

71. READING FACES

"Knowing Signs," "Taking Note."

701 *undying:* unchanging, undrying.
notes: understands.

the unsaid: the unspoken thoughts of the king.

702 *the heart:* the heart-and-mind, one's inner thoughts and feelings.

to the gods: to a god, to divinity, to godliness.

703 *who see behind faces:* "who understands inner thoughts through inner thoughts," "who understands inner thoughts through outer gestures." Parimēlaḻakar interprets this as understanding the movements of other minds by understanding the movements of one's own.

make them your own: "bring them among your limbs," "bring them among your organs," "bring them among the elements of your kingdom."

704 *the same:* the same as others.

705 *see behind faces:* see the note to kural 703.

706 *The fullness of one's heart:* "what is filling one's heart," "what is filling one's mind."

708 *see within:* see and understand what is happening in one's heart. Parimēlaḻakar extends this to being able to remedy what is lacking in one's heart.

It is enough to face them: no words are needed. One need only to stand and be seen.

709 *If one finds those:* should a king gain advisors.

72. KNOWING AN AUDIENCE

Audience: assembly, gathering of the learned.

711 *words:* "the powers of words," "the properties of words."

with care: having considered deeply, having given a matter ample thought.

712 *the occasion:* the most suitable moment.

with clarity: having understood deeply, having come to clarity.

words: "the ways of words," "the ways words move."

713 *words:* "the powers of words," "the properties of words."

strength: capacity, ability.

those speaking: "those endeavoring to speak."

714 *chalk:* white plaster, mortar. Although it does not produce light, it reflects it.

simplicity: simplicity of mind, tenderness. The word's root suggests both the color white or plainness and a tree that lacks a solid inner core.

716 *from grace:* from the way of virtue.

719 *speak well:* "convey well," "deliver well," " drive matters home."
before the wise: among the wise, in the assembly of the wise.
before the little: among the little, in the assembly of the little.

720 *Ambrosia:* as in kurals 11 and 64, the nectar of the gods that yields eternal life.

73. NOT FEARING AN AUDIENCE

Audience: assembly, gathering of the learned.

721 *They never falter:* "their mouths never slacken," "their mouths never fail."
ways: both the ways of an audience and the ways one can falter.
words: "the powers of words," "the properties of words."

722 *convey:* "convey," "deliver," "drive home."

723 *battlefield:* "the place of enemies."

724 *attain:* "take to heart," "learn."
those greater: those greater in learning.

725 *The art of argument:* "the way of measure." Maṇakkuṭavar interprets this to mean knowing the measure of books, which he divides into four kinds: books that investigate the nature of truth, books of scripture and holy writ, books on agriculture and economics, and books on law and warfare.

726 *wise listeners:* "a discerning assembly," "an audience of subtlety."

730 *gone:* "as good as gone." Equal to the dead.
the hall: the court, the assembly.
learning: "what they have learned."

74. COUNTRY

Maṇakkuṭavar groups kurals 74–75 into a subsection on the nature of economy and wealth.

731 *union:* "the uniting," "the coming together." Country as a dynamic and living harmony.
yields: harvests.
untarnished: "untarnished," "unflagging."
people / Of wisdom: people whose character is fitting, proportional, and good.

732 *flourishing:* "thriving," "yielding." Country as a continual giving forth.
wealth: "great wealth," "boundless wealth."
735 *outlaws:* "deadly outlaws," "outlaws that kill."
737 *safety:* a strong fortress, a fortified capital.
740 *if everything fits:* if a country has all the necessary qualities.

75. FORTRESSES

742 *shining water:* "jewel-like water." Sources of water that never go dry, even under the bright summer sun.
stunning: "beautiful." Implicitly, dangerous.
743 *Authorities:* "books." Authors, experts.
safety: fortress. The word in Tamil means both.
744 *with little to defend:* with few or no vulnerable points.
enemies: "besieging enemies," "attacking enemies."
745 *hold:* stand firm, remain strong.
747 *besiege:* encircle.
storm: "attack without encircling."
deceit: treachery within.

76. THE MAKING OF WEALTH

751 *wealth:* "substance," "learning," "meaning," "thing."
worthless: "without substance," "without learning," "without meaning," "nothing."
worthy: "of substance," "of learning," "of meaning," "something."
753 *darkness:* often interpreted as "enmity" or "enemies."
unfailing: "unfailing," "undying," "truthful," "true."
754 *pleasure:* love.
aright: "knowing the right method," "knowing the proper way."
756 *wealth claimed:* wealth that lacks heirs and thus comes to the king.
757 *mercy:* grace, compassion. See chapter 25.
760 *one who is solid in wealth:* one who makes wealth that is solid like the core of a great tree.
wealth that shines: glorious wealth, virtuous wealth, wealth that does not shrink in substance or stature.
The other two: virtue and love.

77. THE SPLENDOR OF ARMIES

"The Splendor of Armies," "Splendor for Armies."

761 *highest:* "chief," "head."
Full of all force: complete and composed of all necessary components.

762 *long lineage:* tradition, generations of experience.

763 *rats:* "an army of rats."

764 *carried / Through time:* born of generations of experience.

765 *death:* the god of death.

766 *assurance:* the support and approval of the king.

767 *Advancing fully in force:* setting out full-fledged, regaled in garlands.
withstanding / Advances: "having learned how to withstand an army's advances."

768 *glory:* splendor. An army may triumph by appearance alone.

769 *smallness:* shrinkage, desertion.
ceaseless aversion: the state of mind leading to rape and looting, scorned by kings.

78. THE VALOR OF WARRIORS

Warriors: "Warriors," "Troops," "Forces."

771 *stone:* memorial stone.

773 *the fallen:* those in danger.

774 *his spear:* "the spear in his hand." Since the spear he had in his hand is gone, he searches for another and is delighted to find one sticking out of his body.

776 *Battle wounds:* wounds to the chest or face.

777 *fame:* "fame that spreads."
the band / Of a warrior: the metal anklet worn by a warrior.

778 *fear death:* "fear for their lives in danger," "fear for their lives in battle."
do not shrink: do not shrink in their nature, do not shrink in their greatness.

780 *king:* "the one who protects," "the one who preserves."

79. FRIENDSHIP

Maṇakkuṭavar groups kurals 79–83 into a subsection on the nature of friendship.

781 *friendship:* given its context in this verse, this chapter, the chapters that follow, and the book as a whole, we can see that Tiruvalluvar is referring specifically to the friends and allies of the king. And yet, as with so many of the book's verses, that very specificity flows outward.
against foes: "against actions." Implicitly, against the actions of foes.

782 *wise souls:* people of wisdom, people of goodness. The word here for wisdom in Tamil not only means "quality," "wisdom," and "goodness" but also, revealingly, "water."

783 *relating to:* "relating to," "moving with."

784 *thunder:* see kurals 447, 448, and 607.

785 *presence:* continual interaction in person.
birth: affiliation by birth into the same community or country.
right: the liberties afforded by friendship.

787 *When / Trouble comes:* if trouble that cannot be averted, as from a god or from fate, appears.
stays: shares in the suffering.

788 *a garment as it slips:* the image implicit in the original is of a garment that has been wrapped and tied around the body and is starting to come loose.

789 *unwavering:* "unwavering," "unhesitating."
Support: "grounded solidity."
in all ways: "in every way possible."

790 *Saying:* "saying," "extolling," "praising," "adorning with speech."

80. EXAMINED FRIENDSHIP

791 *Friends:* "those who embody friendship," "those who have mastered the art of friendship."
cannot flee: "there is no leaving," "there is no release."

793 *undying / Relations:* "the undiminishing community," "undiminishing relations." The entire circle of extended family to which one becomes joined in friendship.

794 *Even by giving:* even by giving something they need; even with gifts.

795 *scorn:* "thunder."
Bring tears: speak so as to bring tears of remorse.
set right: impart knowledge of the right path.

796 *It measures:* "it is a rod that measures."
torment: misfortune, ruin.
merit: benefit, decisive strength.
797 *avoiding:* "avoiding and having nothing to do with." In the Tamil, Tiruvalluvar stretches the last vowel sound in the word for "avoid," as if to show how far one must go.
798 *flees:* "cuts from the way."
shrinks heart: diminishes effort, kills enthusiasm, reduces clarity of thought.
799 *it burns:* "its memory burns the heart."
800 *the unfit:* "the friendship of those unfit," "those out of harmony with the world" (Parimēlaḻakar), "those not equal to one" (Maṇakkuṭavar).

81. LONG FRIENDSHIP

801 *liberty:* the right to act even without asking in advance and to do even what a friend may not like.
This verse takes the accent off time and places it instead on freedom (Parimēlaḻakar).
802 *duty:* "duty," "responsibility," "nature."
wisdom: "the wise."
803 *cannot take:* cannot stand, cannot abide (Parimēlaḻakar).
804 *the great:* the wise, the knowing. The ones who "take them with pleasure" are unspecified in the Tamil, but as Parimēlaḻakar notes of Tiruvalluvar, "Since only the wise would take pleasure in knowing such things have happened, he is speaking of them."
Take them with pleasure: take them as desirable, even if the great wouldn't otherwise desire them.
805 *If a friend offends:* "if friends do something that is painful."
806 *friends in friendship:* friends who remain true to the bounds of friendship.
Faithful over time: true to long friendship.
807 *who love friends:* "whose friendship has come by love."
808 *free:* "strong in the liberty," "able to take the liberty."
Not to hear: not to listen to talk of.
809 *The wise:* "the world." See the note to kural 27.
810 *those / Who don't love them:* implicitly, enemies.

82. HARMFUL FRIENDSHIP

811 *goodness:* "goodness," "character," "quality," "nature."
seem essential: seem entirely lovable. Literally, "seem like those who drink," "seem like those who devour," as in seeming to be absorbed or immersed in friendship.

813 *lovers for pay:* "takers of what's given," "receivers of what's gained." Implicitly, those who take money for love.

816 *grasping:* thick, smothering, all-embracing.

818 *those insisting the possible is impossible:* those who refuse to help when they can.

819 *whose words and deeds never meet:* "whose words are one thing, deeds another."

820 *harsh in public:* publicly dismissive, publicly berating.

83. FALSE FRIENDSHIP

821 *to be struck:* "to be struck when the best moment appears."

822 *of two minds:* who appear to be one way but are thinking another. Contrast with kural 974.

823 *Do not become:* "rarely become," "hardly become," so rare and so hard as to be virtually impossible.

824 *hearts / That scowl:* "hearts that do not smile," "hearts that do not laugh." Hearts that intend harm.

825 *do not meet:* do not correspond with, achieve no harmony with.

826 *One knows quickly:* "one knows quickly," "one must realize quickly."

828 *hands in prayer:* prayerful hands; hands with palms pressed together, as in worshipful greeting.

829 *delighting:* "doing things that bring delight."
feign love: make a great show of friendship.

830 *not heart:* "cast out friendship within," "keep friendship out of one's heart."

84. FOLLY

Maṇakkuṭavar groups kurals 84–95 into their own subsection on the nature of hardship and suffering.

832 *unfit / For one's hands:* unfit for one's station, unfit for one's way in the world.

833 *work:* "work," "task," "labor," "profession."

834 *advises:* "advises others," "preaches to others."
835 *seven lives:* see the note to kural 62.
836 *without skill:* "without hands that know," "without knowing the proper way."
837 *fortune:* "great fortune," "great wealth."
840 *wise company:* the assembly of the wise.

85. PRESUMPTION

"Being Ruled by Paltry Knowledge."

841 *wisdom:* "the world." The community of the learned and wise.
842 *tavam:* in the sense of past good action yielding fruit in the present.
843 *hard:* that is, impossible.
845 *pretending / To:* "conducting oneself as if possessing."
846 *exposed:* visible because uncorrected.
Puts on a fig leaf: "hides nakedness."
847 *wise counsel:* "rare knowledge," "precious teachings."
848 *nor see for themselves:* nor see for themselves the right course of action.
plague: a plague the earth can scarcely bear (Parimēlaḷakar).
849 *the sightless:* not the blind but those refusing to see.

86. DISCORD

851 *unnatural division:* "the division that is the lack of true nature," "the division that is the lack of quality," "the division that is the lack of character."
all lives: all living beings.
852 *Highest:* "chief," "head."
853 *light:* renown.
disease: "woeful disease."
857 *The bitter:* those of malicious knowledge who bring harm to themselves and others.
860 *bitterness:* afflictions, evils.
peak: pinnacle, wealth, exultation.

87. SPLENDOR FOR ENEMIES

"Splendor for Enemies," "The Splendor of Enemies."

861 Compare with kural 250, addressed to renunciants.

862 *enemies:* "the strength of enemies."
863 *friendless:* "one without associations." Unable to connect with others.
864 *Easy:* easy to take.
Who cannot keep secrets: "who has no fullness." Who cannot remain filled with what one knows and is not meant to be shared.
865 *seek no way:* do not follow the way of goodness and virtue.
all chances: all opportunities to enact goodness and virtue.
866 *hostility:* "lack of welcome," "lack of care," "lack of protection."
hosted: "hosted," "welcomed."
868 *virtue:* character, quality, nature.
869 *Joy:* the joy of victory.
870 *fools:* "those who have not studied," "those who have not learned."

88. KNOWING AN ENEMY

871 *kindlessness:* "lack of nature." Not being true to kind.
872 *those who plow with bows:* kings.
873 *Madder:* "poorer," as in poorer in reason and knowledge.
874 *kindness:* being true to kind, being true to one's nature.
Lives: "lives," "endures," "persists," "exists."
light: "greatness," "excellence," "quality."
875 *alone:* "without friends," "without support."
a dear friend: "sweet support."
876 *Whether trusted or not:* implicitly, in times without trouble.
one: implicitly, an enemy.
877 *nor woes:* "nor speak of one's woes."
878 *Perceive:* perceive one's situation.
879 *cut:* "kill."
880 *One breath:* "one only breathes."

89. ENEMIES WITHIN

"Enemies Within," "Inner Enmity."

881 *become bitter:* become hateful.
when bitter: when bringing disease.
882 *fear enemies:* "fear bonds with enemies."
884 *Great misery:* many causes for misery and discord.

886 *If oneness disappears:* if discord appears, if enmity appears.
887 *fit nothing:* both fit nothing themselves and fit no one else.
888 *it:* "its strength."
889 *seed:* "sesame seed."

90. NOT SCORNING THE GREAT

891 *might:* Parimēlaḻakar describes this as the power to carry out whatever one begins.
892 *great suffering:* "unending suffering," "irremediable suffering."
from the great: see kural 29 on the powers attributed to ascetics.
failing to respect: "conducting oneself without respecting."
893 *those above:* "the strong," "the mighty." See the note to kural 891 on "might."
In this translation I follow Maṇakkuṭavar's interpretation. Parimēlaḻakar, by contrast, interprets the verse this way:

> *If one seeks death heed no advice and scorn*
> *Those able to destroy*

894 *summoning:* "beckoning with one's hands."
death: the god of death.
895 *cruel:* "cruel," "severe," "mighty," "burning."
896 *recover:* "escape."
Who scorn: "whose conduct scorns."
The commentator Paritiyar likens the first kind of recovery to the way a tree's roots may escape from a fire to bring forth new shoots in time.
897 *What good are:* "what good is a life of."
898 *to tower:* "to have standing on earth."
899 *the highest in virtue:* those of the highest principles, those of the highest vows; saints, ascetics.
900 *allies:* "allies," "support," "protection."

91. YIELDING TO WIVES

This chapter may appear particularly at odds with modern sensibilities, but one may use it to explore not the question of wives (or of any other kind of beloved) but the nature of yielding, craving, fearing, and following.

901 *No virtue in:* no goodness arises from.
902 *without care:* without regard for goodness and virtue.

903 *losing / Oneself:* "stooping and losing one's own nature."
904 *glory:* "the next life." Glory in the next life.
Gains no mastery of deeds: attains no praise for his actions in this life.
906 *bamboo shoulders:* shoulders and arms that are even and smooth to the touch.
907 *servility:* "servility to one's wife," "conduct always deferring to one's wife."
908 *follow:* defer always to.
wives' brows: "she with a good brow," "she with a beautiful brow." A traditional Tamil epithet for a beautiful woman.
909 *virtue:* "virtuous deeds," "acts of virtue."
wealth: "great wealth."
pleasure: "the remaining action," the third in this set of three.
910 *mind:* heart-and-mind.
in place: in its proper place, in its proper state. This also carries the sense of prosperity, the result of being at work.
at work: at one in one's work. Literally, "with one's heart joined with one's thoughts."

92. LIMITLESS WOMEN

The word here in Tamil for "limit" can mean "limit," "measure," or "marriage." The title thus implies "courtesan" or "prostitute." However, the focus of the chapter isn't so much on these women as on the men who seek them out.

911 *well-bangled women:* "those of choice bangles." Here a term of praise becomes a wry comment on motivation.
912 *heartless:* "without quality," "without nature," "without character."
heart: quality, nature, character.
913 *gripping:* "embracing," but in the sense of one taking care of dead bodies, gripping and carrying whatever their duty requires.
Some corpse: "some unknown corpse."
in the dark: "in a dark room."
915 *The wise:* those of cultivated intelligence.
good minds: natural intelligence.
917 *hearts:* hearts-and-minds.

918 *Without sense:* "who do not discern," "who do not look into things."

919 *arms:* "soft arms," "delicate arms."
jewels: "fine jewels," "excellent jewels."
heedless men: "heedless reprobates," "heedless scoundrels."

920 *fortune:* the goddess of fortune.
of two minds: Contrast with kural 974.

93. NOT DRINKING

The specific drink referred to in this chapter is toddy—palm wine—which stands for alcohol more generally.

921 *Drowning in drink:* "conducting themselves always in love with drink." The Tamil phrase contains the word meaning "to conduct" or "to flow," suggesting that love of drink causes one's life to flow out of one's control.

924 *vile:* "great and despised."

925 *to be out of one's head:* "to not know one's body," "to not know the truth."
way: "hand," in the sense of what fits a person's hands to do. Right conduct.

928 *No use saying:* "give up saying."
hidden: "hidden in one's heart-and-mind."

929 *Arguing with:* "showing reasons to," "giving reasons to."

94. DICE

Gambling.

931 *dice:* playing at dice.

932 *players:* "dice players."

933 *roll away:* "end up away," "end up outside." Parimēlaḻakar interprets this to mean "end up in the hands of enemies."
roll dice: "call the rolling dice."

935 *dice hands:* skill at dicing.

936 *bellies never fill:* in this life.
torments torment them: in the next life.
woe: the goddess of misfortune, Lakshmi's older sister.
of dice: "that is dice."

937 *to the table:* "to the dice hall."
old wealth: ancestral wealth.

938 *makes a person a lie:* "makes one take up falsehood."
939 *takes to tables:* "takes up dicing."
light: renown.

95. MEDICINE

Both the practice of medicine and what serves as medicine.

941 *too little or too much:* traditionally interpreted in one of two ways. The first sees "too little" and "too much" as referring to the trio of elements directly. An imbalance among them, in this view, is what causes disease. The second sees "too little" and "too much" as referring to such things as food, sleep, or activity. In this second view, lack or excess of any of these things is what causes the three elements in turn to cause disease.
the trio / With wind: wind, bile, and phlegm.
named by authors: named by authorities, named by the authors of traditional medical texts.
942 *eats:* "takes care to eat."
after digestion: "after what was eaten is gone."
943 *knowing one's limits:* knowing the right measure of food for one's body.
944 *hunger:* "great hunger," "complete hunger."
946 *moderation:* Parimēlaḻakar describes this as "eating a little less than could be eaten."
947 *fire:* the heat of digestion.
949 *Time:* time, season, moment.
doctors: singular in the original, "the one who has studied."
950 *preparer:* both the one who makes the medicine and the one who gives it.

III. ALL ELSE

96. LINEAGE

This kural opens the third and final section of part II, kurals *96–108*. *Lineage:* traditionally interpreted to mean "birth in a noble family," but as Tiruvalluvar himself suggests, this is a more complicated matter than it may at first appear.

951 *born to a home:* traditionally interpreted to mean "born to a noble family." However, it is equally possible to understand the

word "home" in a more wide-ranging sense and to recognize that a person may be born in many ways. See kural 960 or kural 973 in the chapter on greatness.
morality: "morality," "integrity," "ethics," "uprightness."

953 *cheer:* cheerfulness, laughter, a smile.

954 *Do nothing demeaning:* take no action that would demean themselves. Those who take such actions call into question the nature of their family and birth.

955 *Does not fall from:* "does not fall from," "does not depart from." The phrase in Tamil combines "head" and "separating," as if to suggest a head coming loose from a body, or losing one's sense of direction.

956 *family:* "family," "lineage," "community," "tradition." A different word than in kurals 952–955.

957 *the bright moon above:* "the moon shining prominently in the sky."

958 *the birth / Of a man:* a man's birth in his family, lineage, community, and tradition.

959 *reveal the soil:* "reveal what lies in the soil," "reveal the nature of the soil."
words spoken: "words from one's mouth."

960 *family:* "family," "lineage," "community," "tradition."

97. HONOR

Parimēlaḻakar classifies honor among the qualities belonging to those of a lineage. That is why, in his view, this chapter follows the previous one.

961 *diminishes:* implicitly, diminishes honor.

964 *hair fallen from one's head:* of no account.
place: "place," "station," "state," "status."

965 *the most minuscule diminishment:* "a diminishment the size of a kuṉḏri seed," the kuṉḏri seed being very small.
Mountains: "those like mountains."

966 *name:* renown in this life.

967 *standing:* true to one's standing, remaining in one's station.

968 *guarding:* "living by guarding."
remedy: "remedy," "medicine," "ambrosia." Remedy against death.

969 *the deer that dies / If one hair gets lost:* a mythical deer that dies if it loses even one hair.
970 *Worships:* "worships," "praises."

98. GREATNESS

The qualities of greatness.

971 *Aspiration:* "aspiration," "abundance," "exuberance," "drive." The same word is translated in kural 600 as "strength overflowing." *glory:* light, renown.
972 *born / Of great deeds:* "stemming from the difference in action undertaken." See also kural 26, to which Parimēlaḻakar makes reference throughout his commentary to this chapter.
973 *even high:* even located above. *Even low:* even located below.
974 *one mind:* integrity. Contrast with kurals 822 and 920. *ruling oneself:* "conducting oneself with care."
975 *the impossible:* "those actions that are rare," "those actions that are difficult." See kural 26. *Rightly and fully:* in the proper way.
976 *know:* "know," "experience," "feel." *desire:* "aim," "aspiration."
977 *insolent action:* action beyond bounds.
978 *adores:* "is amazed by."
980 *shields failings:* conceals the shortcomings of others, speaking of their virtues instead.

99. INTEGRITY

The command of noble qualities realized in abundance (Parimēlaḻakar).

981 *what fits:* what matches, what suits, what is natural for a particular person and situation. The word here in Tamil is often translated as "duty" but here refers not to a duty that is externally imposed but to an order discovered in the very nature of things. *natural:* the same word translated in the first line as "what fits." Here, too, everything good—every good quality—comes not from an external sense of duty but from an inner sense of rightness and what fits a particular person and situation.

982 *Goodness:* "goodness," "excellence," "beauty," "quality."
good / Beyond all other goods: "no other good can be called good."
983 *kindness:* see chapter 22 and the note to kural 211.
bedrock: "bedrock," "mainstay," "pillar," "support."
984 *Tavam:* see chapter 27.
not killing: "the good of not killing."
not speaking ill: "the good of not speaking ill."
985 *with it:* "it is the tool with which," "it is the weapon with which," "it is the force by which."
986 *Even against unequals:* in the same manner against one's inferiors as against one's superiors (Parimēlaḻakar).
987 *those not doing good:* those who wrong one.
988 *strength:* "strength," "power," "solidity," "certainty."
Poverty: "not having," "lack," "want."
989 *time:* "time," "eon," "age," "world."
990 *lose their integrity:* "shrink in their integrity."

100. HAVING KINDNESS

Kindness: "Kindness," "Nature," "Quality," "Character." Throughout this translation, the word "kindness" has been used to render several different but related words in Tamil. In this chapter, "kindness" refers not simply to the sense of being helpful or gentle but also to the deeper and root sense in English of being true to kind—being true to one's nature—and acting accordingly. See also kural 874.

991 *openness to all people:* being approachable to everyone. See also kural 386.
the practice / Of kindness: "the practice that is called having kindness." One can also translate "practice" as "way."
992 *the way of kindness:* "the way that is called having kindness," "the practice that is called having kindness."
993 *in limbs:* in body, in outward form.
kindness overflowing: "kindness that abounds," "a nature that abounds," "qualities that abound."
994 *the world:* the community of the learned and wise.
their kind: their nature, their quality.
995 *The kind:* "those who know nature," "those who know qualities." Those who know the natures and qualities of others.

remain kind: remain filled with the qualities of kindness.
997 *as sharp:* as keen in perception and intellect.
without human kindness: without human qualities.
are blocks of wood: lack all human sense.
998 *wrong:* "what is not good," "what is not loving."
last: least in virtue, most unfitting.
999 *those who cannot smile:* "those who cannot smile," "those who cannot laugh," "those who cannot move happily with others." The result of lacking kindness.
1000 *milk:* "good milk."
by its jug: "by the fault of its jug," "by the impurity of its jug."

101. FRUITLESS WEALTH

1001 *gathered:* with the sense of filling up one's place or house.
without tasting it: without partaking of it, without enjoying it.
1002 *grasping:* "grasping without giving."
ugly: "without excellence," "without greatness," "without dignity." Morally ugly.
1003 *hungry:* rapacious.
1004 *One no one loves:* one with wealth who gives nothing to anyone.
1005 *billions:* billions on billions.
1006 *give:* "give something," "give anything."
Parimēlaḻakar interprets this verse as saying that the one who won't enjoy his wealth and give something to the worthy is a disease to his wealth, since he prevents it from fulfilling its nature.
1007 *great goodness:* great goodness and beauty without and within.
1008 *one unloved:* one with wealth who gives nothing to anyone in need, even if they live right beside him. See also kurals 216, 217, and 1004.
square: "in the center of the village," "in the center of the town."
1009 *all wealth:* "shining wealth," "splendid wealth," "beautiful wealth."
Without . . . enjoyment: "by suppressing oneself," "by blocking oneself," as one might block the flowing of water.
1010 *rain:* "rain," "water," "clouds."

102. HAVING MODESTY

Modesty: the word in Tamil can also be translated as "shame," but it is the disposition against doing anything shameful rather than the experience of shame itself.

1011 *Modesty in action:* disposition against doing anything shameful.
brows: see the note to kural 908.
1012 *such:* "the rest." The other key elements of life.
1013 *bodies:* "flesh."
integrity: "integrity," "goodness," "virtue," "excellence."
1014 *pride:* "a proud gait."
affliction: disease.
1015 *fear:* shrink from, would be ashamed by. See kural 428.
shame: see the chapter note.
the wise: "the world."
1016 *want:* "want," "seek," "desire," "cherish."
The wide world: the astonishing world.
1018 *Virtue itself feels shame:* virtue, ashamed, abandons him.
1019 *family:* "family," "lineage," "community," "tradition."
1020 *modesty:* "modesty within," "modesty in their hearts."
puppets: "wooden dolls."

103. SERVING FAMILY

"Ways of Family." The ways that allow a family to thrive.

1021 *in action:* that has begun an action.
I won't ever cease: "I won't rest my hand." I won't cease till I've completed that action.
1022 *Mastery of action:* see chapter 62.
thriving: "thriving in action," "thriving in deeds."
1023 *sets forth:* "comes forward."
1024 *success:* the successful completion of one's aims.
Obtains: happens of its own accord.
1025 *the wise:* "the world." The community of the learned and wise.
1026 *To command:* "to take command of." To raise up one's family.
1027 *those able:* those able to act.
1028 *Dally in pride:* "delay and think of one's honor."
it's gone: one's family falls.

1029 *are they only / Vessels for suffering:* implicitly, no. These bodies are vessels for greatness.
1030 *upright:* "upright," "standing."

104. FARMING

"Plowing" but encompassing all the arts of agriculture.

1031 *Turn as it will:* no matter where the world may turn.
the world: the community of the learned and wise.
highest: chief, head.
1032 *pin:* linchpin.
world: "the people of the world."
1033 *honor them for food:* "honor and eat," "praise and eat." Depend on them for their lives.
1034 *many shelters:* "the shade of many umbrellas." The umbrella here stands for the king's umbrella, which grants cooling shade to his subjects. Hence, implicitly, many kings.
their king's shelter: "their umbrella." Their king's umbrella.
Those whose fields shelter grain: "those with the quality of shade who have grain." Those growing grain who are gracious and generous. Maṇakkuṭavar describes them as "those who have shade without umbrellas," noting that, along with supporting themselves, farmers can also make their kings thrive.
1035 *He who eats:* "he whose nature is to eat."
1036 *fold their arms:* fold up their hands, refuse to work.
I need nothing: "I've renounced all desiring."
1037 *dries it:* leaves it to dry, leaves the land fallow.
flourishes: yields abundantly.
1038 *Better than:* more important than. Plowing and water, though, still remain good.
watching: "watching," "protecting," "guarding."
1039 *husbandman:* the word in Tamil means "farmer," "husband," and "lord." For an exploration of the meanings of "husbandman" in English and its relation to a similar system of analogies that connect agriculture, marriage, and the sacred, see the work of Wendell Berry and his essay "Discipline and Hope," first published in *A Continuous Harmony: Essays Cultural and Agricultural.*
stays away: does not visit it, does not walk it.

105. WANT

"Want," "Destitution." In Parimēlaḻakar's definition, the utter absence of anything to enjoy or experience.

1041 *want:* "having nothing."

1042 *Want:* "having nothing."

1043 *loveliness:* beauty in body, speech, and standing.

1044 *born to a family:* see chapter 96.
want: "having nothing."
despair: the slackness of energy that leads to negligence.

1046 *know:* understand fully.

1048 *lack:* "lack," "poverty," "penury," "destitution."

1049 *poverty:* "poverty," "lack," "penury," "destitution."

1050 *Death to gruel and salt:* cause of the exhaustion of the gruel and salt of others.
let go: "renounce completely," "let it all go." See chapter 3.

106. BEGGING

"Begging," "Entreating," "Soliciting."

1051 *Seeing:* if you see.
refusing: if they refuse.
fault: "fault," "shame," "wrong," "vice."

1054 *deny nothing:* "do not know refusing," "do not know concealment."

1055 *Because some on earth deny nothing:* "because those who deny nothing exist on earth."
stand in sight begging: beg by merely standing in view.

1056 *Seeing those:* one need not even beg.
woe of withholding: Parimēlaḻakar calls this an illness, because withholding belies a lack of wholeness.

1057 *Seeing people:* one need not even beg.

1058 *puppets:* "wooden dolls." Since people would no longer accrue the goodness of giving, they would be as good as dead.

1059 *splendor:* renown, glory.

107. DREAD OF BEGGING

Fear of begging, of entreating, of soliciting.

1061 *eyes:* "people like eyes," people as precious as eyes.
that delight in giving: "that hide nothing and delight in giving."

1062 *perish:* "perish completely," "be utterly undone."
1063 *hardship:* "the hardship of poverty," "the misery of having nothing."
1064 *with nothing:* "with no place."
Nothing: "no place."
1065 *broth:* "a thin broth," "a thin gruel."
1069 *wilt:* "melt," "shrink."
1070 *passes:* goes, leaves him.

108. WICKEDNESS

In this final chapter of part II, Tiruvalluvar deals with the opposite of "The Splendor of Kings" with which he began.

1071 *no others / Look:* "we have seen none who look."
1073 *Do:* "conduct themselves by doing."
1075 *code:* code of conduct, code of honor, rule of life. Fear keeps villains in line and is their way in the world.
and avarice / A little if there: literally, "beyond that, if avarice is there, there is a little [in this code]."
1077 *wet hands:* hands wet with food, hands newly washed after eating.
1078 *respond to:* are of service in response to.
crushed like cane: crushed and wrung like sugarcane.
1079 *Seek out their faults:* "are expert at seeing their faults." See faults even when they have none.
1080 *rush:* if they didn't move quickly, people would realize their wickedness and not buy.

PART THREE LOVE

Of the three parts of the Tirukkural, this may be the most Tamil. It draws on a long tradition of Tamil love poetry, which in turn draws on the Tamil landscape and on a series of figures and situations intertwined with that landscape. One may find a point of entry in A. K. Ramanujan's celebrated *The Interior Landscape: Classical Tamil Love Poems.*

In Parimēlaḻakar's arrangement, the twenty-five chapters of part III fall into two sections: secret love (kurals 109–115) and wedded love (kurals 116–133). Secret love could also be translated as "clandestine love" or "stolen love." The chapters, however, can also be categorized in other ways. To the attentive reader, the verses offer their own clues.

I. SECRET LOVE

109. ALLURE

The bewildered experience of the lover seeing his beloved.

1081 *siren:* "siren," "celestial woman," "deity."
jewels: "beautiful jewels," "beautiful earrings."

1082 *sirens:* see the note to kural 1081.

1083 *death:* "that which is called death."
fierce: "fierce," "warring," "battling."

1084 *don't fit:* "are warring against," "are battling against."

1086 If her eyebrows were straight, they would hide her eyes and I would not suffer her gaze.

1087 *An elephant:* "an elephant in rut," "an elephant in rage."

1088 *forehead:* brow. See the note to kural 908.

1089 *all these jewels:* "these mismatched jewels," "these clashing jewels."
this doe-eyed girl: this girl with eyes as innocent as a deer's.

110. KNOWING SIGNS

1092 *Furtive:* "secret," "unseen." Seemingly unseen.
love: romantic love, erotic love, lovemaking.

1094 A verse that exemplifies Tiruvalluvar's understanding of love's subtleties. If the love-stricken young man isn't looking at her, how can he see she's smiling?

1096 *sees:* "understands quickly," "sees quickly."
Parimēlaḻakar attributes these words to the heroine's girlfriend, who speaks them to herself.

1097 *seem cross:* "like those of enemies."

1099 *Looks:* "common looks," "general glances."

111. THE JOYS OF JOINING

Joining: "being together," "embracing," "uniting."

1101 *this shining jewel:* she with the shining jewels.

1103 *lotus-eyed god:* "the one with lotus eyes," interpreted as Tirumal (Vishnu), Indra (Lord of the Gods), or saints and ascetics more generally.

1104 *cools:* delights. In Tamil, rooted in a land that blazes in summer, coolness evokes delight and pleasure.

1106 *ambrosia:* as in kurals 11, 64, and 720, the nectar of the gods that yields eternal life.

1107 *golden:* beautiful; shining in complexion; the color of dried mango leaves.
like feasting with guests / In one's home: the stage of the householder, not yet attained.
Parimēlaḻakar attributes these words to the hero, answering the heroine's girlfriend who tells him, "You should marry her quickly and make a home."

1108 Parimēlaḻakar attributes these words to the hero, who refuses the advice to marry given by the heroine's girlfriend. Where there are not two, how can there be marriage?

1109 *Turning:* "turning cold," "sulking."
joined in love: Parimēlaḻakar interprets this as joined in marriage.
As in kurals 1107 and 1108, Parimēlaḻakar attributes these words to the hero, who refuses the advice, given by the heroine's girlfriend, to get married. Marriage leads to the cycle of turning cold and turning back again. We have no need of this, for we are one in love already.

1110 *this jewel:* this beautifully jeweled one.

112. IN PRAISE OF HER

1111 *anicham:* see the note to kural 90.

1112 *anyone:* "many."

1113 *smile:* her teeth as revealed by her smile.
her arms—bamboo: see the note to kural 906.

1114 *water lilies:* "the blue lotus," "the purple water lily," "the blue nelumbo."
look to the ground: "droop and look at the ground."

1115 *good drums:* drums of celebration instead of drums of mourning.
anicham: see kurals 90 and 1111.
His beloved's waist is so slender that even the weight of an anicham flower with its stem would be too much for it to bear.

1120 *Anicham:* see kurals 90, 1111, and 1115.
berries of thorns: the thorny nutlets of *Tribulus terrestris*, sometimes called cow's thorn or bullhead in English.

113. IN PRAISE OF LOVE

The first five verses speak in the voice of the hero, the second five in the voice of the heroine.

1123 *my eye:* "the pupil of the eye."
brow: see kurals 908 and 1088.

1124 Parimēlaḻakar paints a picture of the hero saying these words to himself as he leaves his love's side, having noticed the arrival of dawn.

1127 *I do not paint them:* because to paint them I'd have to close them, even only for a moment.

1129 *if I close my eyes:* if I sleep, awaiting his return.
place: "place," "town." Implicitly, friend, girlfriend.
With the hero staying away, the heroine does not sleep, which leads her girlfriend to call him heartless. But the heroine clings to his image in her eye. Compare with kurals *1219* and *1220*.

1130 The hero has gone away and people call him heartless. For the heroine, however, he remains in her heart. Compare with kurals 1219 and 1220.

114. DOWN WITH DECORUM

"Casting Off Shame." In ancient Tamil Nadu, a lover made his love public, in hopes of marriage, by mounting a horse made out of palm leaves and pulling an image of his beloved behind him.

The first seven verses speak in the voice of the hero, with the remaining three in the voice of the heroine.

1131 *those suffering love:* those who have loved in secret and suffer from separation in public.

1132 *decorum:* shame, propriety. The lover has already lost all of his other strengths and virtues. This is the only one that remains.
soul: "life," "breath," "spirit."
palm: the palm-leaf horse.

1133 *power:* "power," "mastery," "energy."
proportion: modesty, propriety, a sense of shame.

1134 *proportion and power:* see the note to kural 1133.

1135 *palm:* the palm-leaf horse.

1138 *pity:* pity for my state.

thought: thought of my honor, thought of my virtue.

1139 *Love:* the heroine treats the love she has as its own being or entity.

115. TALK

The importance of knowledge conveyed by gossip. With the once secret lovers exposed and apart, such talk keeps their hearts connected.

The first five verses speak in the voice of the hero, with the second five in the voice of the heroine.

1141 *People talk:* people talk of our love.
dear life continues: my aching but precious life remains alive. Some commentators also interpret this phrase to mean that the hero's beloved remains alive.
grace: "divinity," "fortune," "luck."
Many don't know this: if they did, they wouldn't talk, and dear life would cease living.

1142 *so rare:* so precious, so hard for me to reach.
place: "town," "people," "community."
talks / And gives her to me: for such talk keeps anyone else from marrying her.

1143 Parimēlaḻakar sees this verse and the others from the first half of this chapter as what the hero says to the heroine's girlfriend, who has come to tell him the rumors and urge him to get married.

1144 *die:* "lose its nature."

1146 *once:* "one day."
A snake swallowed the moon: image for a lunar eclipse.

1147 *talk:* "the talk of this place," "the talk of this town."
illness: lovesickness.

1149 *said not to worry:* said not to worry that he'd leave me.

1150 *do right:* "grant," "give," "bestow." Marry me, take me with him. Maṇakkuṭavar interprets this verse as saying, instead, that since this place has talked, its people will now give me to him.

II. WEDDED LOVE

In Parimēlaḻakar's arrangement, kurals 116–133 fall under the heading of wedded love, exploring the archetypal figures and situations of Tamil love poetry pertaining to married life.

116. UNBEARABLE ABSENCE

The agony experienced by a heroine when her husband has to go elsewhere to work or to fulfill some other obligation. This agony is often described by the heroine's girlfriend rather than the heroine herself, as if to show that even the thought of his departure leaves her speechless.

1151 *if coming back quickly:* if you're saying you'll be coming back soon, as you go out the door.
Tell those still living: because I'll already be dead.
Parimēlalakar interprets this kural as spoken by the heroine's girlfriend to the hero, in which case the line would mean "for she'll already be dead."

1152 *His sight:* even just seeing him.
His touch: "our embracing," "our uniting."
Notice how this kural takes on different tones if one hears it as the voice of the heroine or as the voice of her girlfriend.

1153 *His words:* his promise to remain, his words of consolation.
he knows: he knows she can't bear his absence.
But parting still looms: but somehow he still plans to go.
Here, too, this could be either in the voice of the heroine or in the voice of her girlfriend.

1154 *If he says not to worry:* if he says, "Don't worry, I'm not leaving."
those who believed: the heroine's girlfriend speaks of her friend and herself as if they were other people.

1155 *reunion:* "union," "embrace."

1157 *This captain:* "the one of the harbor," "the one of the seaside," "the chief of a maritime tract." In traditional Tamil love poetry, the seashore is associated with the agony of separation.
Here the heroine says to her girlfriend, "You needn't tell me he's going; my body already withers away." See also kural 1234.

1158 *live without sisters:* "living where there are no sisters," "living in a place without any girlfriends." Since you didn't keep him from going, you aren't a sister of mine. Here I have no sisters.

1159 *which burns when touched:* which burns only when touched.
1160 *their hearts healed:* "having cured their lovesickness."
there are so many: implicitly, there are none.

117. PINING AWAY

1162 *nor tell it:* since her husband is away, she would need to send him a message and doing so would bring her shame.
1163 *Love:* lovesickness.
hang from the ends: the image is of a pole balanced on one's shoulders, each side bearing its own burden.
1167 *In love's vast waters:* "swimming in love's vast waters."
1170 *thoughts:* "mind," "heart-and-mind."

118. THE LONGINGS OF EYES

1171 *ails me:* "that caused this unending ailment."
1172 *eyelined eyes:* eyes that had beauty but not knowledge.
saw without seeing: saw without knowing, saw without realizing.
suffer without seeing: suffer without seeing how they caused their own suffering.
1174 *eyelined eyes:* see the note to kural 1172.
This endless disease: "this endless, unbearable disease."
1175 *illness:* "lovesickness."
1178 *Cannot rest without seeing him:* one might go so far as to say that her beloved has actually returned, but her eyes, worn out from weeping, can neither see him nor bear not seeing him.
1179 *he comes they don't sleep:* they remain awake out of fear that he'll leave again.
1180 *drums for eyes:* eyes that broadcast everything.

119. PALLOR

1181 *how I've paled:* "how my nature has paled," "how my nature has sallowed."
1182 *he gave love:* "he gave." He gave me love, he gave me himself, he gave me myself.
1185 *there:* the there between here and far way.

120. THE ANGUISH OF SOLITUDE

1191 *Those having:* implicitly, I am not among them.

1192 *rain:* implicitly, rain in measure, as opposed to unseasonal or ruinous rain.
Without the gift of her love's presence, the heroine feels like a field without rain.

1193 *lovers who are loved:* lovers who have their love with them.
glory: "glory," "exultation."
Since she and her husband are apart, the heroine experiences life as death.

1194 *Those loved:* those loved and respected by all.

1195 *what does the one / We love give us:* only suffering.

1196 *Like a pole:* like a pole on one's shoulders.
Parimēlaḻakar encapsulates the sentiment this way: "If he felt the love I feel, would I be suffering like this?"

1197 *Standing:* standing and conducting himself.
love: the god of love.

1198 Parimēlaḻakar sees this verse as spoken by the heroine who still hasn't seen the messenger she sent return.

1199 Parimēlaḻakar also sees this verse as spoken by the heroine who still hasn't seen the messenger she sent return.

1200 *Dear heart:* "bless you, heart."
sea: the sea of love, the sea of suffering.

121. THE LONGING OF MEMORY

1201 *The thought alone:* even just thinking of when we were together.
sweeter than wine: see kural 1090.
Parimēlaḻakar sees these words as the words of the hero, speaking to his friend who acts as his messenger. Other commentators see the verse as the heroine speaking to her girlfriend.

1202 As with kural 1201, Parimēlaḻakar sees this verse as coming from the hero, speaking to his friend who acts as his messenger. Maṇakkuṭavar, by contrast, sees it as the heroine speaking to her girlfriend, answering her friend's fear that this desolation will ruin her.

1203 The kural refers to the thought that people sneeze because someone is thinking of them.

1204 Parimēlaḻakar suggests that the heroine wonders in this verse whether her love hasn't returned because he hasn't finished his work, even though he remembers her, or because he has and has forgotten her.

1206 *our days:* "our days together."
Both Parimēlaḻakar and Maṇakkuṭavar see this verse as the heroine's answer to her girlfriend, who says, "All this thought of him is killing you."

1207 *thought:* the thought of being apart, the thought of forgetting him.

1208 *he never gets angry:* because he doesn't care, because he doesn't love me.
how great / My lover's regard: like a great ascetic, he shows compassion even for my faults.

1209 *cruelty:* "lack of compassion," "lack of benevolence."

1210 *I would see him:* Parimēlaḻakar writes that when lovers apart both see a bright moon, their eyes touch each other in that gaze.
Without leaving: without leaving my heart.
Maṇakkuṭavar interprets the phrase "Stay and shine" as "Go and set" or "Why won't you set?" In his interpretation, the heroine wants to sleep so she can see her love in her dreams.

122. TALK OF DREAMS

The heroine tells her girlfriend what kind of dreams she's been having.

1211 *message:* "message," "messenger."
what: "what welcome," "what feast."

1212 *carp-like eyes:* eyes darting like carp; eyes swimming in tears.

1213 *no love:* no heart or compassion, for he hasn't yet returned.
in life: in waking life.

1214 *Dreams give me love:* "love exists because of my dreams."
bring: "find and bring," "seek and bring back."
no love: no heart or compassion, for he hasn't yet returned.
in life: in waking life.

1215 *in life:* in waking life.

1216 *If there wasn't this waking:* "if there wasn't this thing called waking."

1217 *brute:* "cruel one," "harsh one."

without love: heartless and compassionless, for he hasn't yet returned.

1218 *He's back in my heart:* "he has rushed back into my heart."

1219 *call him:* "condemn him as," "accuse him of being."
loveless: heartless and compassionless, for he hasn't yet returned.
in life: in waking life. Compare with kurals *1129* and *1130*.

1220 *These people:* "the people of this place," "these neighbors." Compare with kurals *1129* and *1130*.

123. THE MISERY OF EVENING

In classical Tamil love poetry, evening is associated with the anguish of separation.

1221 *the lance that ends wives:* "the lance that devours the lives of wives."
live long: "bless you." Curse you.

1222 *bless you:* see the note to kural 1221.
bewildering: Parimēlaḻakar sees this in reference to evening being neither day nor night.

1224 Implicitly: With my beloved the evening arrived and brought me the joys of life.

1225 *evil:* "enmity," "hostility."
the evening: the evening that brought the joys of union during the time that the heroine and her beloved were secretly together.
the dawn: the morning that brought the pain of separation during the time that the heroine and her beloved were secretly together. Now it brings instead the memory of dreaming.

1226 *him:* "my love," "my husband."

1227 *At dawn:* see the note to kural 1225.
this disease: this lovesickness.

1228 *Battle-axe:* "weapon of death."
evening ablaze: "evening that burns like fire."

1229 *sorrow / Will baffle this place:* because I'll be dead.
this place: this village, this town.

1230 *who thinks only / Of wealth:* whose nature has turned only toward wealth.

124. THE DROOPING OF LIMBS

1231 *shy even from flowers:* compare with kural 1114.
Parimēlaḻakar interprets this verse as said by the heroine's girlfriend, who takes her friend's plight so much to heart that she speaks of them both as being left in sadness.

1232 Parimēlaḻakar interprets this verse as said by the heroine's girlfriend, implying that the heroine must get ahold of herself.

1233 Parimēlaḻakar interprets this verse as said by the heroine's girlfriend, implying once again that the heroine must get ahold of herself.

1234 *are losing their bangles:* "slacken and lose their bangles," "lose their greatness and bangles."
Parimēlaḻakar interprets this verse as said by the heroine's girlfriend, implying yet again that the heroine must get ahold of herself.

1235 Parimēlaḻakar interprets this verse as said by the heroine's girlfriend, implying a final time that the heroine must get ahold of herself.

1236 One can imagine this as the heroine's reply to her girlfriend's words in kural 1235.

1237 *the uproar of my arms:* "the uproar caused by my arms."
The heroine's heart wants to go to the hero. See also chapter *125*.

1238 *brow:* see kurals 908, 1088, and 1123.
Parimēlaḻakar interprets this verse as said by the hero to himself. If that could happen when I held her in my arms, what might this absence do to her?

1239 *One puff of air:* see also kural 1108.
Parimēlaḻakar interprets this verse as said by the hero to himself. If that could happen as we embraced, what might this absence do to her?

1240 *forehead:* see kurals 908, 1088, 1123, and 1238.
Said by the hero to himself.

125. TO HER HEART

1243 *woe:* "disease," "distress," "affliction."

1244 *take / My eyes with you:* when you go to see him.

1245 *hate him:* "call him an enemy," "call him despised."
leave him: "release from our hand."

1246 *who soothes:* "who embraces and soothes."
1248 *loveless in ignorance:* loveless not knowing how we suffer.

126. LOSS OF RESTRAINT

Steadiness, self-control, adherence to principle.

1251 *aching:* "love," "passion," "eros," "desire."
1252 *Love:* "aching," "passion," "eros," "desire."
1254 *Escapes into the open:* "escapes and stands in public."
1255 *dignity:* greatness, restraint.
1257 *he:* "the loved one," "the lover," "the beloved."
1258 *forces:* "forces," "powers," "armies," "weapons."
modesty: "womanhood," "womanliness."
The sweet nothings: "the many gentle lies."

127. LONGING TO REUNITE

Parimēlaḻakar sets the first seven kurals in the voice of the heroine and the last three in the voice of the hero.

1261 *grow weak and lose luster:* from watching and watching for his return.
1262 *Glittering friend:* "you adorned in bright jewels." Implicitly, you with no idea, you who have done nothing to help me. Commentators see this verse as the heroine's answer to her girlfriend, who tells her to forget about her love.
if I forget him: "if I forget him now," "if I forget him today."
forever: now and in lives to come.
1263 *With his heart:* with his heart as his companion and not me. "Heart" can also mean "mind" or "intention."
I'm still here: I still exist.
1264 *He:* "the one who left."
with love: with the same love we knew together.
1265 *him:* "beloved," "husband."
1266 *illness:* "lovesickness that causes one to pale."
1268 *I shall dine:* I shall return home and feast.
1270 *hold:* embrace, unite with.
one's heart: for Parimēlaḻakar, "her heart"; for Maṇakkuṭavar, "my heart."

128. MAKING SIGNS KNOWN

1271 *dark eyes:* eyelined eyes.
Parimēlaḻakar interprets this verse as said to the heroine by the hero, who has returned.

1272 *bamboo-armed:* see kurals 906 and 1113.
Parimēlaḻakar interprets this verse as said by the hero to the heroine's girlfriend.

1273 Parimēlaḻakar interprets this verse as said by the hero to the heroine's girlfriend.

1274 Parimēlaḻakar interprets this verse as said by the hero to the heroine's girlfriend.

1275 *her bangles:* "her closely placed bangles."
Parimēlaḻakar interprets this verse as said by the hero to the heroine's girlfriend.

1276 *passion and fire:* "greatness" and "rareness."
Tell me they'll disappear: "tell me of lovelessness." Tell me he's leaving again.
Parimēlaḻakar interprets this verse as said by the heroine to her girlfriend.

1277 *coolness:* the coolness of separation.
lover from cool shores: see the note to kural 1157.
my bangles / Know it before I do: they already slip from my arms. See also kural 1234.
Parimēlaḻakar interprets this verse as said by the heroine to her girlfriend.

1278 Parimēlaḻakar interprets this verse as said by the heroine to her girlfriend.

1279 *her bangles her arms:* because her bangles are already slipping from her arms gone lean.
her feet: because they want to go with you.
That's what she did: that's what she did upon realizing you were going; that's what she did upon my telling her you were going.
Parimēlaḻakar interprets this verse as said by the heroine's girlfriend to the hero.

1280 *tell:* "tell and implore." Ask without asking for what heals their lovesickness: the presence of their beloved.

129. LONGING FOR UNION

Parimēlaḻakar interprets the first seven verses as the heroine's answers to her girlfriend who says, "If you think he'll be leaving again, why aren't you angry?"

1281 *Rejoicing:* gleefulness, inebriation.
not wine: see kurals 1090, 1145, and 1201.

1282 *tree:* "palmyra tree."
seed: "millet seed."
The same pairing appears in kurals 104 and 433.

1283 *without care:* without care for me, without caring for me.

1284 *went / To his side:* went to join him, went to embrace him.

1285 *him:* "husband."

1287 *knowing the current:* "knowing the water will take him."

1288 *Despite your disgrace:* "though you do things that bring disgrace."
Parimēlaḻakar sees this as the heroine's girlfriend speaking to the hero. Maṇakkuṭavar sees it as the heroine addressing him directly.

1289 *moment:* "moment," "season," "occasion," "apex."
Parimēlaḻakar places this kural in the voice of the hero. Maṇakkuṭavar places it in the voice of the heroine.

1290 Both Parimēlaḻakar and Maṇakkuṭavar place this kural in the voice of the hero.

130. AT ODDS WITH ONE'S HEART

1296 *thinking:* thinking of him, thinking of how he wronged me.

1299 Parimēlaḻakar sees this kural as the voice of the hero. Maṇakkuṭavar sees it as the voice of the heroine.

1300 *kind:* kin.
Parimēlaḻakar sees this kural as the voice of the hero. Maṇakkuṭavar sees it as the voice of the heroine.

131. SULKING

The first of the three chapters on sulking that bring the Tirukkural to a close.

1301 Both Parimēlaḻakar and Maṇakkuṭavar see this as the voice of the heroine's girlfriend, giving the heroine her advice.

1302 *Sulking is like salt:* a little sulking, like salt, brings out the sweetness of love.
Both Parimēlaḻakar and Maṇakkuṭavar see this as the voice of the heroine, in answer to her girlfriend's advice.

1303 Parimēlaḻakar sees this as the heroine speaking directly to the hero.

1304 *turning / To:* "reconciling with," "being conscious of," "experiencing," "realizing." See also kural 1109.
turned away: turned away in feigned anger, turned away out of hurt.
As with kural 1303, Parimēlaḻakar sees this as the heroine speaking directly to the hero.

1305 Sulking is beauty for the good because sulking leads to reunion.
Parimēlaḻakar sees this as the hero speaking to himself, having reunited with his love, who had been sulking.

1306 *quarrels:* the quarrels of old grievances.
sulking: the sulking of new grievances.
rotten or unripened: Parimēlaḻakar associates the rotten fruit with quarreling and the unripened fruit with sulking.
Parimēlaḻakar sees this as the voice of the hero. Maṇakkuṭavar sees it as the voice of the heroine.

1307 Both Parimēlaḻakar and Maṇakkuṭavar see this as the voice of the hero.

1308 *sees that one suffers:* sees that one suffers because of him or her.
Parimēlaḻakar sees this as the voice of the hero. Maṇakkuṭavar sees it as the voice of the heroine.

1309 *Sulking in love is sweet:* "sulking with one who loves is sweet." Implicitly, sulking with one without love is bitter.
water / In shade is sweet: cool water in shade quenches one's thirst, unlike water beneath the hot sky.

1310 Here I've followed Parimēlaḻakar, who sees this verse as the voice of the hero. By contrast, Maṇakkuṭavar sees this as the voice of the heroine. His reading could be translated like this:

> *One able to let me keep wasting away—my heart*
> *Yearns only to join him*

132. SULKING'S SUBTLETIES

1311 *women:* "all women," "all those with the nature of women."

1313 *a garland of new flowers:* "a garland of tree flowers." Parimēlaḻakar notes that since sulking, in Tamil poetry, is associated with the fields, this garland of tree flowers, coming from somewhere else, heightens his wife's sense that he wears them for someone else.

As Maṇakkuṭavar puts it, even to adorn myself is wrong.

1314 *our love is greater than any:* we love more fully than anyone has ever loved.

Which any which any: which other woman have you been with that our love exceeds?

1315 *Overflowed with tears:* thinking we'll part in the next.

1316 *I remembered you:* I thought only of you when I was gone, I remembered you always when I was gone.

forgot: The implication is that if he hadn't forgotten her, he couldn't have remembered her, because to remember one must first forget. See also kural 1125.

As Maṇakkuṭavar puts it, even to have thought of her is wrong.

1317 *sneeze:* the belief is that people sneeze because someone else thinks of them. See also kural 1203.

As Maṇakkuṭavar puts it, even to sneeze is wrong.

1318 *Whose thought do you hide:* "do you hide the thought of one of your lovers?" See also kurals 1203 and 1217.

As Maṇakkuṭavar puts it, even not to sneeze is wrong.

1319 *calm her:* calm her after sulking, reassure her after sulking.

As Maṇakkuṭavar puts it, even to reassure her is wrong.

1320 *think:* think upon all of her qualities.

Who do you think of: whom do you compare me to.

As Maṇakkuṭavar puts it, even to look at her is wrong.

133. SULKING AND BLISS

1321 *Brings:* "is a powerful way to make."

closer: more loving, more caring.

1322 *sag:* "sag," "droop," "wilt."

1323 *joined like earth and water:* compare with kural 452.

heaven: celestial realm; realm of gods; heavens.

For those versed in classical Tamil literature, this kural, like kural 64, evokes a poem from one of the ancient anthologies, in this case Kuṟuntokai. The author of the poem is known simply as Cempulappeyaṉīrār, "Honored of Rainfall and Red Earth," which refers to a line from the poem itself:

Who is your mother to mine
How is my father related to yours
How did we know one another
Like rainfall and red earth
Our hearts themselves came together

1324 *open:* "break open," "break down."

1325 *something:* joy, sweetness, pleasure.

1326 *having eaten:* "digestion of what was eaten." The sense is that the hunger once a meal has been digested makes the next meal all the more sweet.
loving: "joining," "coming together," "uniting."

1328 *forehead:* see kurals 908, 1088, 1123, 1238, and 1240.

1329 *long:* long enough to yield sulking's sweet fruit.

1330 *joy of joys:* "even a greater joy than that." In Parimēlaḻakar's ordering, the last word of this verse ends with the last sound of the Tamil alphabet, just as the first word of the first verse of the first chapter begins with the first sound of the alphabet. Here I've tried to give my own small nod to that.

ACKNOWLEDGMENTS

My first and largest debt is to the late Dr. K. V. Ramakoti. Without his years of patient teaching and encouragement, I would never have dared to take on this project. I am also deeply indebted to his late wife, Mrs. K. R. Padmavathi, and to all of their family and extended family for their long hospitality and friendship.

Heartfelt and tender thanks go as well to twelve other late friends whose encouragement and example remain as alive as ever: Hayden Carruth, John Berger, Sam Hamill and Gray Foster, William and Paula Merwin, Kamala Surayya, Subba Raju, Paul L. Love, K. P. C. Pitchai, David Citino, and Norman Care.

Happily, I'm still able to cherish the worldly presence of twelve other friends who have helped me in this effort more than I can say: C. F. John and Reena Kappen, Wendell and Tanya Berry, Gustavo Esteva and Nicole Blanco, Vidya Bhushan and Prabha Arora, Uma and Ashis Nandy, Joe-Anne McLaughlin-Carruth, and Robert Longsworth.

Scholarships and fellowships from Oberlin Shansi, the US Fulbright Program, Ohio State University, Oberlin College, and the National Endowment for the Arts have all aided this project enormously, and I am grateful for the time and support they offered.

I am also grateful for the unwavering support of my parents, sister, and brother-in-law, who have stood by me through many strange-seeming decisions and borne my many long absences from home.

If I were to try listing all the friends and well-wishers in Tamil Nadu and in India who have helped me learn Tamil over the past two decades, I would not only run out of space but also run the risk of inadvertently leaving someone out. I do, however, want to acknowledge the village of Valayappatti, whose people have shown me how the ideals of the Kural continue to be embodied in actual life. To all of my family and neighbors in that place, my deep and enduring thanks. And to all of my friends in Madurai, Tamil Nadu, and beyond, my unending gratitude and appreciation.

For their insights and assistance during the final revisions of the poems and preface, my appreciation to Martha Selby, David Shulman, and Paula Richman. For miraculously finding a home for this translation in the middle of a pandemic, a deep bow to my agent, Malaga Baldi. For seeing and supporting the possibilities of this project, joyful thanks to my editor, Amy Caldwell, and to all of her extraordinary colleagues at Beacon Press. For her illuminating introduction, my immense appreciation to fellow translator and scholar Archana Venkatesan. And for his insightful and timely foreword in a tumultuous time, my gratitude to Andrew Harvey.

Finally, without the love and support of my husband, David Mielke, I would never have found the energy to continue what has sometimes felt like a never-ending apprenticeship. If this translation can hope to touch people's hearts and lives, it is because he has deeply touched mine.